Mexicocina

Mexicocina

THE SPIRIT AND STYLE OF THE MEXICAN KITCHEN

Photographs by Melba Levick

Text by Betsy McNair

CHRONICLE BOOKS

SAN FRANCISCO

For my dear friend and agent, Sarah Jane Freymann, because she loves the kitchen. But especially because of her friendship, professional acumen, and unending support throughout the years.

M. L.

For Jane, who opened the door to Mexico, and Joan, for the spirited welcome.

E. E. M.

Library of Congress Cataloging-in-Publication Data:

Levick, Melba.

Mexicocina : the spirit and style of the Mexican kitchen / photographs by Melba Levick ; text by Betsy McNair.

p. cm.

Includes index.

ISBN-10: 0-8118-4528-1
ISBN-13: 978-0-8118-4528-1

1. Kitchens—Pictorial works. 2. Kitchens—Mexico—History. 3. Cookery, Mexican. I. McNair, Elizabeth. II. Title.

TX653.L464 2006

747.7'970972—dc22

2005031584

Manufactured in China

Designed by Viola Sutanto

Distributed in Canada by Raincoast Books
9050 Shaughnessy Street
Vancouver, British Columbia V6P 6E5

10 9 8 7 6 5 4 3 2 1

Chronicle Books LLC
85 Second Street
San Francisco, California 94105

www.chroniclebooks.com

page 2. The striking blue-and-white zigzag tiles are a traditional Moorish pattern brought to Mexico by the Spanish. The stove itself is a modern adaptation of the traditional Mexican wood-burning stove, brought up-to-date with the installation of gas burners. Firewood was stored under the arch below, and the fire was lit in the area under the grills, here decoratively tiled, and used to store griddles.

Contents

Introduction

above. In Zinacantan, Chiapas, a young Maya girl cooks tortillas on a clay *comal* over a wood fire, just as her ancestors did thousands of years ago.

In my research for *Mexicocina,* I was quite often met with a bit of confusion. Spanish speakers would answer my queries about *cocinas mexicanas* with an enthusiastic litany of ideas about the many wonderful cuisines of Mexico. "No, no, no," I would say, "I'm looking for the beautiful kitchens of Mexico; it's a book about the kitchens themselves." For, you see, in Spanish the word *cocina* means both "cuisine" and "kitchen." This gave me pause, and as I traveled through Mexico visiting the homes, inns, cooking schools, and museums that house the forty glorious kitchens celebrated in these pages, I realized that this dual translation provided the perfect context in which to view those kitchens—to look deeply into the evolution of Mexico's cuisine through the ages in order to see how it has influenced and directed the design and style of the Mexican kitchen. I believe that the spirited and stylish kitchens represented in *Mexicocina* eloquently express that connection.

Before the Spanish came to the Americas, the indigenous people living in what we now know as Mexico enjoyed a predominantly vegetarian diet based on a holy trinity of beans, corn, and chiles. Cultivated gardens provided avocados, squash, tomatoes, and herbs. Fish and game were plentiful; insects added protein as well. As they had for thousands of years, they used flat and hollow grinding stones carved from volcanic rock (*metates* and *molcajetes*) to grind chiles and corn. Potters worked clay into plates and cups for eating, a flat round griddle (*comal*) for cooking tortillas, and pots (*ollas*) for simmering beans and stews. Most cooking needs were met by a kitchen hearth of three rounded rocks on the floor, a fire blazing inside.

The arrival of the Spanish in 1519 brought years of military conquest, one omnipotent god, and a variety of new tastes to the table. Beef, milk, cheeses, rice, olives, wine, onions, and wheat augmented the indigenous cuisine, necessitating new cooking methods, utensils, and kitchen designs. Ovens for baking bread appeared where once a *comal* had sufficed for making tortillas. Now wide hearths in which to roast meats and simmer stews were built against the wall, where once a pit oven (*pib*) was used. Chocolate, historically a spicy bitter drink imbibed only by royalty, was now a sweet concoction enjoyed by many, requiring special cooking pots and a wooden whisk (*molinillo*) for frothing. Potters from Talavera de la Reina, Spain, immigrated to Puebla and began to fill the New World with their high-fire, double-glazed ceramics (*talavera*). In time, galleons from the Far East brought foods and merchandise from exotic lands—spices, silks, fruits, fine porcelain—further influencing the flavors and kitchens of New Spain.

These myriad influences blended with existing indigenous foods and cooking customs, the exact mix differing from region to region, depending on geography, climate, and ethnicity. On the Yucatán Peninsula, the foods of indigenous Maya acquired Caribbean and Mediterranean flavors due to their location on the Gulf Coast. In Puebla, arguably the most European city in New Spain, a sophisticated cuisine developed, typified by its most famous dish, *mole poblano,* in which native turkey was cooked in a complex sauce of Old World spices blended with New World chiles and chocolate. The diverse regional cuisines of Mexico were emerging.

Colonial convents and monasteries played an important role in this evolution of cuisine and kitchen. Their substantial financial resources and social standing gave them access to many of the new ingredients arriving in New Spain, and their kitchens became the laboratories of this developing fusion cuisine. Also, the unlimited free labor provided by the natives "in exchange" for religious instruction allowed them to construct the most sophisticated and beautifully designed kitchens of the day, setting the standard for upper-class homes. Often these convent kitchens consisted of several separate rooms, one for each of the tasks now performed regularly as part of this new cuisine—a cool room in which to age and store meats and cheeses, a room for tortilla making, a smoke house. In the main room of the kitchen, a new cooking surface appeared: a raised hearth, usually built against the wall, with grates set into the top and a wood or coal fire burning in the firebox below. This new "stove" allowed for better temperature control and facilitated the handling of heavy pots. Walls were hung with clay pots of many sizes (*ollas* and *casuelas*) for cooking rice, beans, and sauces, copper kettles (*cazos*) for making candies, and decorative racks filled with practical wooden utensils. Wooden closets (*alacenas*) and shelves (*trasteros*) were built to hold dishes and glassware. Aqueducts brought water to tiled basins near the stove; by 1717, in fact, the kitchen of the Convent of Santa Rosa in Puebla had hot and cold running water. In the kitchen garden, cabbages, turnips, and citrus fruits now grew alongside tomatoes, chiles, and time-honored medicinal herbs. Rituals and incantations to the gods of fire, water, and corn disappeared as the nuns prayed to San Pasqual Bailón, the Christian saint of kitchens and cooks.

In 1815, after three centuries of Spanish rule, Mexico achieved independence from Spain, politically if not gastronomically. A brief period of French reign from 1864 to 1867 heightened the Eurocentric appetites and manners in the upper crust of society (made up of *peninsulares,*

above. Locally produced *talavera* tiles adorn the floor, walls, and alcoves of the Santa Rosa Convent in Puebla.

above. *¡Viva Frida!* At Hotel Casa Vieja in Mexico City, a self-portrait by the artist/activist Frida Kahlo is reproduced on a refrigerator in one of the inn's lovely suites.

Spaniards born on the Iberian Peninsula, and *criollos,* people of pure Spanish blood born in the New World), but it was during the thirty-one-year dictatorship of President Porfirio Díaz, beginning in 1876, that French styles in architecture, the arts, and cuisine pervaded Mexico. By then gas stoves had appeared in the upper-class kitchens of Mexico City and other prosperous cities, beginning a gradual replacement of their wood- and coal-fired predecessors. Breads and pastries made with white flour and sugar competed with tortillas for a place at the Mexican table. Dining moved out of the kitchen and into a separate room, and in the affluent homes of the era, candlelight meals were served on magnificent tables topped with fine linens from Europe and set with *talavera* from Puebla, crystal from Catalonia, silver from Taxco, and delicate porcelain from China—tangible evidence of the hybridization of cultures that had taken place, for those who could afford it.

The mix of cultures was complex, its problems equally so. The economic gap between the rich and poor was vast, and even greater was the social gap between those of Spanish descent—*peninsulares, criollos,* and now the *meztizo* (mixed race)—and the poor Amerindians. Church and state were at odds, liberals and conservatives couldn't agree, and even in the kitchen a chasm existed between the elite's taste for wheat and the maize-based diet of the natives. The rifts that plagued Mexico eventually led to ten years of civil war. By 1920 a new democracy was formed, and with it came a revitalized Mexican nationalism—*Mexicanidad*—honoring all things pre-Hispanic, from art and architecture to couture and cuisine. Frida Kahlo and Diego Rivera, along with other artists, poets, and freethinkers of the time, were at the vanguard of this movement, and at Casa Azul, Frida's childhood home, where she and Diego now resided, they expressed their nationalist pride with collections of folk and pre-Hispanic art. Frida delighted in the indigenous clothing she wore and in the authentic dishes she served from her thoroughly traditional kitchen. No longer a colony, free from the oppression of the landed gentry, a new self-directed Mexico began to look to her native roots.

On the gastronomic front, culinary researchers began to track traditions deep into the hills and valleys of the vast republic, where a rich trove of regional Mexican cuisines was quietly thriving. Though processed foods, soda pop, and nutrition-free white bread managed to invade the Mexican pantry during the second half of the twentieth century, and an electric blender took the place of the *molcajete* on most Mexican kitchen counters, Mexico's regional cuisines became the passion of many, including a dynamic group of women chefs in Mexico City, the Círculo Mexicano de Arte Culinario, who dedicated themselves to preserving and promoting Mexican regional cuisine. And interestingly, one of the most passionate crusaders for traditional Mexican cuisine is not Mexican, but an Englishwoman, Diana Kennedy. For the last fifty years,

Diana has made it her mission to document authentic Mexican recipes from across the republic, and she shows no signs of slowing down as she traverses the country in search of yet another unrecorded recipe or fabled cook. Her seven seminal cookbooks are the backbone of recorded Mexican gastronomy. Today, talented chefs across Mexico and the United States trained in this rich culinary heritage forge the future of *la cocina mexicana* for an ever-broadening and enthusiastic audience.

Hand in hand with this heated passion for Mexican cuisine, of course, comes fresh interest in the other *cocina Mexicana,* the traditional kitchen of Mexico. In the past two years, as we traveled through Mexico photographing and researching the kitchens featured in this book, we were constantly reminded of this growing enthusiasm. Across Mexico, haciendas are being lovingly brought back to life, their kitchens repaired and renovated by owners with an astute awareness of the place in Mexican history these haciendas hold. The museums of Mexico are impressive by any standard, and the great number of them that include kitchens is significant, reflecting both the kitchen's intrinsic historical value and an impressive Mexican "culinary pride." The timeless design features of these kitchens not only capture the past for visitors, but also continue to inspire the design of kitchens today. In towns like Mérida and San Miguel de Allende, the demand for modern living spaces in harmony with the local colonial style is staggering, and talented local artisans—stonecutters, masons, carpenters, tile-setters, blacksmiths, painters—are adding their age-old handcrafts to these new kitchens, no small feat in our pre-fab world. In every state we visited, we discovered modern kitchens honoring Mexico's past.

It is our sincere wish that our love for Mexico—our affection for the people, our respect for the culture, our appetite for the flavors, and our flat-out enjoyment of the sights and sounds of this fascinating country—shines through in the photographs, words, and recipes found in *Mexicocina.* Whether you're a long-time Mexicophile or a newcomer, we hope that the glorious kitchens featured in this book—the modern kitchens, the public kitchens, the so-small-you-can-barely-turn-around-in kitchens, the very personal kitchens, the zany kitchens, the cooking school kitchens, the colorful kitchens, the historical kitchens, all the kitchens—will inspire you to create your own *cocina Mexicana* wherever you are. *¡Buen provecho y buena suerte!*

above. In Yucatán, ancient Maya designs inspire today's pottery created by A. Mena.

chapter I

An Artist's Eye

Three unique kitchens express the personal visions of Rodolfo Morales, Frida Kahlo, and Deborah Turbeville

RECIPE: FRESH FRUIT DRINK, AGUA FRESCA

Born in 1925 in a humble village in Oaxaca, Rodolfo Morales studied art in Mexico City in the 1940s, where he began a thirty-two-year teaching career at a secondary school upon graduation. He lived and worked in quiet obscurity until fellow Oaxacan artist Rufino Tamayo discovered his work in 1975 at an exhibit in Cuernavaca and introduced his surreal and vivid paintings to a welcoming Mexican—and eventually international—art world. Ten years later Morales was able to retire from teaching and return to his rural Oaxacan village to paint full-time and "live in my memories," as he put it. Rooted in these memories, he filled his canvases with dreamlike images of women, markets, and folklore, all in flamboyant color. Possessed of a truly generous spirit, the quiet man painted profusely, used color liberally, and created a foundation dedicated to preserving colonial architecture, popular arts and traditions, and the ecology of Oaxaca. His studio and home are now open to the public, the playful kitchen there yet another example of the master's inspired art.

Behind walls of vivid cobalt blue in a leafy neighborhood of Mexico City lies Casa Azul, where surrealist artist Frida Kahlo was born, spent her youth, and later lived with her husband, Diego Rivera, until her death in 1954. Subjected to a life of pain and suffering—initially due to illness and a tragic streetcar accident, and later to Diego's perpetual infidelity—Kahlo nonetheless became Mexico's most famous female artist, an icon of artistic self-expression. When a spirited revival of nationalism and pride in cultural traditions took place in Mexico in the 1940s, Frida and Diego were at the forefront of this movement, known as *Mexicanidad.* They filled their home and lives with all things Mexican, and nowhere was Frida's profound *Mexicanista* spirit more evident than in her vibrant kitchen at Casa Azul.

Years ago, walking in her New York City neighborhood, photographer Deborah Turbeville found herself drawn to the Mexican art and artifacts she saw in shop windows and dreamed of someday finding the right setting in which to surround herself with them. Fate stepped in, and she was soon on assignment in central Mexico, where a day-trip to San Miguel de Allende convinced her that she had found her new town and a second visit yielded the perfect house. Over the next few years Deborah and Mexico City designer Patricia Bubela restored the colonial-era house, creating an extremely personal atmosphere that expresses Deborah's artistic esthetic and her love for the collectible art—folk, kitsch, functional, and sacred—that had lured her to Mexico.

opposite. An assortment of wooden spoons and utensils fill a wooden *cucharero* (spoon rack), and various earthenware pots, pans, and pitchers conveniently hang on the kitchen walls.

left, top. Morales painted the doors of this wooden cupboard with the vibrant fruits and vegetables found in his beloved village markets.

left, bottom. Following a long-standing Mexican tradition and taking it to new heights, Morales completely covered the kitchen walls with his collection of cooking pots. Those on the lower left are pure decoration, but the large *casuelas* along the top are used throughout Mexico to cook rice, sauces, and stews.

page 10. Rodolfo Morales's love of boisterous color is evident in his joyful kitchen. Brilliant yellow walls and a striking geometric arrangement of dazzling tiles add to the spirited mix.

page 11. Chiles soak in a blue enamel bowl, softening in water before they are pureed for a Oaxacan *mole. Mole* loosely translates from Nahuatl as "sauce" and has come to mean any of a number of sauces—seven in Oaxaca alone—containing ground chiles and spices.

above. Three classics from the craft villages of Michoacán — a burnished and painted decorative piece between two richly glazed green pots — rest atop the gleaming tiled stove.

left. High on the wall, Diego's name is decoratively spelled out in green and brown glazed cups.

opposite. In her exuberant kitchen, Frida used tiny earthenware cups to form garlands, lovebirds, and to write their names on the walls. A bold geometric pattern of yellow and blue tiles from Puebla covers the width of the traditional wood-burning stove. Aside from the installation of a window that brings in needed light, the kitchen remains exactly as it was when she and Diego resided in Casa Azul.

above. These cream-and-chocolate plates from Tzintzuntzan, Michoacán, are part of Frida and Diego's sizable collection of Mexican folk art they proudly displayed at Casa Azul.

right. Wooden shelves holding ceramics from Michoacán are painted in brilliant yellow, Frida's preferred color. Even the kitchen and dining room floors of Casa Azul are coated in this dazzling shade.

opposite. Frida and Diego's dining room was home to unending gatherings of their famous — and infamous — friends who gathered to discuss their political convictions and to enjoy Frida's celebratory meals, always accompanied by boisterous singing and copious amounts of tequila. The French doors open onto an enclosed courtyard, which Frida filled with lush tropical plants and a small menagerie of beloved pets. Two papier-mâché figures by Carmen Caballero provide whimsical contrast to the formal still life paintings on the walls.

St RAPHAEL
QUINQUINA

opposite. In Deborah Turbeville's central Mexican home four warrenlike rooms of the original house were transformed into a spacious eat-in kitchen, where her eclectic collections fill every corner. A glass cupola adds natural light; the fireplace adds ambient warmth. A talented local artisan covered the stucco walls with layer upon layer of colored washes until the dusky-rose that Deborah envisioned was achieved.

left. A photographer's instincts are evident in the color, shape, texture, and composition of the diverse assemblage of folk art, sacred art, and kitchenware found in this corner of the kitchen.

below. Pots and pans hang from a mesquite beam below a wall graced with *retablos* and ex-votos (devotional paintings, often done on tin, venerating or giving thanks to a particular saint). Inspired by Frida and Diego's folk art on display at Casa Azul, Deborah adorned the kitchen walls with her collection.

Fresh Fruit Drink

Agua Fresca

INGREDIENTS

Makes 1 quart

3 CUPS FRESH FRUIT CHUNKS

2 LIMES, JUICED

3 CUPS WATER

3 TABLESPOONS SUGAR

PINCH OF SALT

Fruit-based "cool waters" are sold throughout Mexico from giant glass jars, their vivid hues as inviting as their luscious flavors. Almost any ripe fruit—cantaloupe, pineapple, mango, watermelon, papaya, and so on—is transformed into a refreshing cool drink by simply pureeing it with water and sugar. Feel free to combine fruits; one delicious blend is pineapple-cucumber.

1. **Place the ingredients in a blender** and puree until very smooth. Chill.
2. **Serve** over ice.

opposite. Small blue-and-white star tiles from the pottery town of Dolores Hidalgo contrast with solid terra-cotta tiles around the stove, adding another layer of visual texture. Larger tiles in the same star pattern line a mesquite beam supporting the *campana* (hood) over the stove, where a kitschy wooden rendering of the Last Supper hangs.

Big Ideas

Smart use of small spaces at Casa Santana, Casa Areca, and Casa Felipe Flores

RECIPE: SPICED MEXICAN COFFEE, CAFÉ DE OLLA

The owners of three very different homes—a gracefully aging manse on the Yucatán Peninsula, a reclaimed ruin near the public laundry in San Miguel de Allende, and a rambling colonial house in the highlands of Chiapas—all confronted the same design constraint when they built or remodeled their kitchens: small spaces in which to fit their grand ideas. Faced with this challenge, the owners devised practical and attractive ways to expand the workability of their kitchens. Creative thinking led to shelves and storage where one wouldn't expect them, cooking areas outside the confines of kitchen walls, and innovative uses of tile and color. These are not minimalist kitchens by any means; the owners of all three have a penchant for Mexican crafts and possess cherished mementos that they weren't about to live without. With a bit of creative thinking, they didn't have to.

At Casa Santana, an inviting guesthouse in Mérida, Yucatán, the artistic proprietress used soft chalky washes of harmonious colors to cover the large surfaces in her tiny kitchen. This subtle palette creates a spacious feel, the perfect background for a few bright bursts of vibrant color in the glassware and ceramics on display in her kitchen.

In San Miguel de Allende, the owners of Casa Areca transformed a crumbling three-hundred-year-old ruin into a lush oasis of greenery, water, and light, wrapping the living spaces around a center courtyard with a retractable roof. The second-floor kitchen provided just enough space for a range, sink, and refrigerator, so they installed a wood-fired grill in the adjacent dining room, where the extra space allows them to cook overlooking their verdant haven, effectively doubling their workspace.

Casa Felipe Flores in San Cristóbal de las Casas encompasses two contiguous houses; one a popular six-bedroom inn, and the other the owners' private home. In both abodes the kitchen space is limited, but colorful tile work and creative storage allow for kitchens filled with treasures gathered during the owners' years of travel in Mexico, as well as prized artwork from their previous life in the United States.

right. It's impossible to feel cramped in a kitchen with eighteen-foot ceilings like those at Casa Santana. The tall French doors leading outdoors, a slow-moving ceiling fan, and cement floor tiles of stunning design keep things cool when summer becomes sultry in Mérida.

opposite, top. Brilliant cobalt-blue glassware from Guadalajara and a coffee and tea set from Oaxaca brighten the shelves above the sink, where they create a striking display when not in use. Cobalt was the first tin glaze used in Mexico, and it remains a classic.

opposite, bottom. Using unoccupied space above the pantry door, the owner's collection of touristware — novelty pottery created in the 1950s for visitors to Mexico — found the perfect home.

page 22. In the diminutive kitchen of Casa Santana local artisans used *cal* (lime) washes of soft ochre, and the walls fairly glow with reflected sunlight from the adjacent courtyard. The wooden doors received a light stain, giving them just a subtle hint of color, and the large windows in those leading to the dining room lead the eye beyond the room's four walls.

page 23. A shelf carved into the twelve-inch-thick wall holds 1950s pottery from Oaxaca. The owner fondly — and accurately — refers to this as "dripware," for lack of an official name. The glorious colors of these ceramics are due to glazes high in lead, making them unsuitable for serving food, but her artful arrangements throughout the kitchen provide visual excitement.

Leche

opposite. At Casa Areca, the earthy colors of copper pots, wooden cabinetry, brick lintels, and a terra-cotta floor harmonize beautifully with tiles of deep sage-green from Artesana, a home decor shop in San Miguel de Allende. The charming "antique" painted doors are a modern creation done by artists in nearby Dolores Hidalgo.

left, top. A brick-trimmed shelf above the stove provides room for the owners' treasures: an heirloom clock, pots garnered during years spent in Guatemala, and kitschy papier-mâché roosters. The hand-painted glazed tiles, classic *talavera* from Puebla, were purchased decades ago and forgotten until recently, when the owner discovered them in his parents' garage. Newly appreciated, they are now the focal point of Casa Areca's appealing kitchen.

left, bottom. The kitchen space was expanded into the dining area with the construction of a wood-burning *parilla* (grill). Aside from adding a striking architectural feature to the room, it is fully functional. Behind the grill is a mural of exquisitely painted tiles done by Capelo, a multitalented artist who resides in the hills between San Miguel and Guanajuato.

above. Even in this small area, there is room for an artistic vignette. Carved pieces — spoons, mermaids, and a tortilla marker on the wall — echo the warm wooden glow of the cabinetry. Ceramic colanders — *pichanchas* in Spanish — are handmade in many rural villages where they are used to rinse *nixtamal,* corn for making tortillas.

opposite. Pure-white china (and daughter Iza's baby plate) fill a simply designed wooden dish rack, which efficiently uses available wall space and is a "lighter" alternative to a closed cabinet. The corncob trivets above act as decoration until called into service.

very well d the evening.
other put h bed.

opposite. At Casa Felipe Flores in San Cristóbal de las Casas, Chiapas, the owners of this welcoming bed-and-breakfast used matching cobalt-and-white tiles to cover everything — walls, countertops, and shelves — in their pint-size personal kitchen. The repetition of color and pattern creates visual uniformity and effectively opens up the space.

left, top. On the left, the blue-and-white plate is *cerámica corriente*, everyday dishware produced throughout Mexico and sold in most markets. The hand-painted platter and gourd bowl on the right are vibrant examples of lacquerware from nearby Chiapa de Corzo, Chiapas. Unpainted gourds are used extensively for storage in the kitchens of Mexico, while painted examples such as these are used for decoration or in celebrations.

left, bottom. Three simple Oaxacan bowls top a brilliant crimson table runner from the village of San Andrés de Larrainzar, an exceptional example of the exquisite weaving done in the highlands of Chiapas. Each color and design holds age-old meaning to the Maya, and every village uses a unique combination of hues and patterns, allowing a visitor to identify the provenance of the piece by its colors and motifs. The intricately lacquered tray is from Olinalá in the state of Guerrero.

above. Bluebirds, thought to bring good luck, adorn these hand-painted tiles from Dolores Hidalgo.

left, top. In the bed-and-breakfast kitchen at Casa Felipe Flores, a tiled arch set into the wall provides useful storage behind the stove as well as an interesting focal point. The owners' collection of plates, from visits to favorite potteries in Guanajuato, Puebla, and Tonalá, repeat the curve.

left, bottom. A funky painted wooden chicken from nearby Guatemala sits atop the tiled counter.

Spiced Mexican Coffee

Café de Olla

INGREDIENTS

Serves 8

- 2 QUARTS WATER
- 3 OUNCES PILONCILLO, OR ½ CUP DARK BROWN SUGAR, FIRMLY PACKED
- TWO 4-INCH CINNAMON STICKS
- 1 CUP DARK ROAST GROUND COFFEE

The name for this strong, sweet, spicy coffee comes from the *olla* (cooking pot) traditionally used in Mexican kitchens to prepare it. Mexican cooks say that the *olla* imparts a subtle but perceptible flavor to food cooked in it.

Before using a new *olla,* you'll need to season it by filling it with water, bringing the water to a boil, and allowing it to cool in the pot. Don't worry if you don't own one; this recipe is still delicious when prepared in a heavy saucepan.

The coffee is sweetened with *piloncillo,* a cone-shaped unrefined sugar found in most Mexican markets, but brown sugar may be substituted. For *café con leche* (coffee with milk), fill the cups only ⅔ full with the coffee, and top off with warmed milk. A splash of brandy or Kahlúa is delicious too.

1 **In a saucepan over medium-high heat,** heat the water, sugar, and cinnamon and stir until the sugar has dissolved. Increase the heat and bring to a boil, then add the ground coffee, stir, and lower the heat to a simmer. Cook for 2 to 3 minutes.

2 **Remove from the heat,** let sit for 2 minutes, and strain the coffee into warmed cups.

chapter 3

La Buena Vida

A glimpse of the good life at Haciendas San Gabriel de las Palmas, Itzincab, Petac, and Calderón

RECIPE: SHRIMP AND MANGO COCKTAIL, COCTEL DE CAMARONES Y MANGO

Part myth and part magic, the historic haciendas of Mexico hold undeniable romantic intrigue. For more than three centuries, these self-sustaining estates functioned much like the plantations of the Southern United States, providing the economic backbone of Mexico. Whether producing sugar, raising cattle, growing agave, or processing silver, they brought untold wealth to Spanish *hacendados* (landowners) and a life of toil to the native workers. Eventually the system had to end, and in 1910 revolutionary heroes Pancho Villa and Emiliano Zapata—crying "¡Viva México!"—reclaimed the land for native Mexicans, leaving a trail of ransacked haciendas behind them. Almost a century later, thanks to the interest of visionary Mexicans and foreigners alike, these estates are being rescued from years of neglect, lovingly restored, and reincarnated as luxury hotels, private homes, and country retreats.

Just an hour south of Cuernavaca lies Hacienda San Gabriel de las Palmas. Constructed by Hernán Cortez in 1529 as a Franciscan monastery, it eventually became the most important sugar mill in Mexico and, ironically, Pancho Villa's headquarters during his crusade to end the hacienda era. San Gabriel now houses a small luxury hotel, allowing visitors to spend the night nestled in Mexico's resplendent past.

Cattle ranches dotted the Yucatán Peninsula during the colonial period, but by the late nineteenth century most had changed over to cultivating henequen, a sisal-like fiber harvested from agave that was used to make rope and twine. Architectural styles evolved as well, and Haciendas Itzincab and Petac represent two stages in this evolution. Itzincab is a neoclassic marvel, testimony to the European tastes of Yucatán's "exalted class" during the late 1800s. Built on the site of a Mayan ruin, Petac retained its colonial bones as it changed from cattle ranch to sisal plantation. In its current incarnation as a private residence available for rent, guests revel in modern luxury housed in an impeccably restored colonial masterpiece.

The romantic storied past of Hacienda Calderón, in the rolling hills outside San Miguel de Allende, includes serving as a battle site during the War of Independence with Spain, a weekend retreat for a Mexican president, the home of a famous Mexican bullfighter, and the setting of a 1956 movie. American interior designer Marcia Brown purchased the abandoned hacienda in 1998, and her tasteful remodel brought new life to the faded beauty, while still preserving its fabled history.

page 34. As was common at the time, the ground floor of Hacienda San Gabriel de las Palmas was used for storage and housing livestock, and the upper floors held the living spaces. In the spacious second-floor kitchen, a grand horseshoe-shaped stove with nine burners provided space for several cooks to work simultaneously as they prepared meals for myriad workers at the hacienda.

page 35. Guajillo chiles shine like burnished leather in a wooden animal bowl from Ixtapán de la Sal.

left. Clay *tasitas* (little cups), glazed in green and brown, outline the fireplace, arches, and still life paintings.

below. Metates and *molcajetes,* both pre-Hispanic kitchen grinding tools, are still in common use today. The tiles seen throughout the San Gabriel kitchen are hand painted with whimsical pictures.

opposite, left. Pantry-scene paintings like this one, known as *bodegones* in Spanish, were extremely popular in colonial Mexico. While they might feature the corn and cacao of the New World in place of the oranges and grapes of the Old, they were nonetheless classic European still lifes. Pottery pieces from Taxco, Guererro, and Michoacán line the hearth.

opposite, right. Scalloped arches known as *conchas* (shells) such as this one above the water cistern were a Mudejar architectural feature often built around doors and windows in colonial Mexico. Their origin is Moorish; the word *Mudejar* refers to Islamic artisans living under Christian rule in Spain.

above. A wide terra-cotta band borders the arch over the recessed hearth in Hacienda Itzincab's original kitchen, circa 1750. Though the current owners added a modern kitchen nearby for their everyday use, this time-honored room remains in its original state, and they often use the dramatic hearth as a backdrop for bountiful buffets when friends and family gather.

opposite, top left. The small cistern on the lower left held rainwater for use while cooking on the wood- and cactus-fired hearth. Fires were built below the grates, and the ashes fell to the bottom, where they were easily removed through the opening at floor level.

opposite, top right. The current owner of the hacienda discovered this basin of *piedra dura* (literally "hard stone" and the name for a common Yucatecan stone) in the garden, where it had once been part of the plantation's irrigation system. Charmed by its simplicity and sense of history, he installed it on a base of similar stone in a corner of the old kitchen. The zigzag orange-and-blue ginger jar is from Dolores Hidalgo.

opposite, bottom. The land surrounding Itzincab is redolent with scented blossoms, and the air hums with wild bees (Itzincab means "place of honey"). Here in the kitchen against a cobalt-blue background, fruits and flowers fill baskets and bowls on the hearth.

Mexico

opposite, top. An antique shelf on the kitchen wall holds cobalt-blue glassware. Beyond a mesquite door, *cal* (lime) washes on the stucco walls of the dining room glow scarlet.

opposite, bottom left. Carved from the trunk of a tree, this wooden *mortero* (mortar), filled to overflowing with fresh colorful fruit, was originally used with a large wooden pestle to grind coffee, salt, and corn.

opposite, bottom right. Architect Salvador Reyes Ríos and designer Josefina Larraín located this decorative piece of pistachio-green molding in an antique store in Puebla. Hung above the stove, it keeps oft-needed utensils nearby.

above. Colorful ceramic canisters from Dolores Hidalgo sit atop the poured-concrete counter.

page 40. In the sunny yellow kitchen of Petac's *casa principal* (main house), the charming staff of local Mayan women prepare Yucatecan specialties and share their recipes with delighted guests. The massive beam above the tile-fronted counter and backsplash was recovered and recycled from the machine house of the old hacienda.

left. During the latest renovation of Hacienda Calderón in 1998, a wall was demolished, doubling the size of the grand kitchen. When the crumbling roof was replaced, numerous skylights were added to bring an abundance of light to the inner rooms of this rambling home.

above. The tiled shelves on either side of the hearth are filled with antiques from a lifetime of collecting. Many are pitchers used for serving pulque, a mildly fermented drink made from the maguey plant that is produced in haciendas throughout Mexico.

opposite, left. Above concrete counters stained terra-cotta red, a simple wooden cabinet holds spices and memories.

opposite, right. Pepe Ortiz, a famous Mexican matador who owned the hacienda in the 1950s, added the distinctive green tile from Dolores Hidalgo to the fireplace. The oversize green bowl is from Patamban, Michoacán.

right. A wooden *trastero* (shelf for dishes) from Michoacán holds a wealth of beautifully crafted dishes collected at flea markets, antiques stores, and small-town markets throughout Mexico.

Shrimp and Mango Cocktail

Coctel de Camarones y Mango

INGREDIENTS

Serves 6

- ¼ CUP FRESH ORANGE JUICE
- ¼ CUP FRESH LIME JUICE, OR TO TASTE
- 2 TABLESPOONS RICE WINE VINEGAR, SEASONED OR PLAIN
- 1 TABLESPOON OLIVE OIL
- ½ TEASPOON SALT, OR TO TASTE
- 30 MEDIUM COOKED SHRIMP, PEELED AND DEVEINED
- 1 SMALL JICAMA, PEELED AND CHOPPED
- 1 RED BELL PEPPER, CHOPPED
- 2 SEEDLESS ORANGES
- 1 RIPE MANGO, PEELED AND CHOPPED
- 2 RIPE AVOCADOS
- ½ CUP FRESH CILANTRO LEAVES

This beautiful and tasty recipe was inspired by a wonderful appetizer served at Hacienda Chichén in Yucatán. Belisa Barbachano-Gordon, granddaughter of the hacienda owners, and a gracious hostess herself, told me that this recipe is an old family favorite, and I can see why. She serves it in stemmed Mexican handblown glassware and even suggests that you drizzle a tablespoon or so of white tequila over it before serving.

One important step in this recipe is chopping the fruits and jicama. It's important to chop them all about the same size—about 1-inch square—so that each bite will have the right balance of flavors.

1 **In a bowl, stir together the orange juice,** lime juice, vinegar, olive oil, and salt.

2 **Place the shrimp, jicama, and bell pepper in a bowl** and pour the juice mixture over them. Toss to coat. Cover with plastic wrap and refrigerate for at least 2 hours and up to 6 hours.

3 **Peel the oranges with a paring knife,** removing the rind and pith. Holding an orange in your hand, slice along each membrane to remove orange sections whole. Cut each orange section in half. Repeat with the second orange and reserve the halved sections.

4 **About one half hour before serving,** pit and peel the avocados and cut the flesh into 1-inch square pieces. Add the mango, oranges, and avocados to the shrimp and toss to coat. Cover and return the bowl to the refrigerator. Chop the cilantro leaves and reserve.

5 **To serve, check the seasoning,** adding more salt or lime juice if you like, and stir in about half of the cilantro. Divide the mixture between 6 glass goblets and sprinkle with a bit more cilantro for garnish.

chapter 4

Folk Art Fever

Mexico's popular art fills the kitchens of Casa Luna, Casa de Jalatlaco, Casa de Cinco Perros, and La Casa de Espíritus Alegres

RECIPE: AVOCADO DIP WITH SEASONAL FRUIT, GUACAMOLE CHAMACUERO

The owners of these four houses are all avid collectors of Mexican folk art, and their kitchens are filled to overflowing with the treasures they've gathered on their travels throughout Mexico. For them, collecting folk art is not just an act of acquiring popular art, but the adventure of traveling the unbeaten path, the magic of the serendipitous meetings, and the personal connection made with an artist.

Some designs relate to the work of the kitchen—decoratively shaped lava-rock mortars and pestles (*molcajetes y tejolotes*) used for grinding; ornately carved wooden spoons, spatulas, and whisks; paintings and statues of San Pasqual Bailón, the kitchen saint; ceramic pots and platters of all shapes and sizes—and some are simply pieces that bring joy to the owners as they go about their daily kitchen tasks, reminding them of hours spent knocking on doors in dusty villages, navigating mountain roads with only a crumpled handwritten map in hand, conversing in a fusion of Spanglish and the unfamiliar local dialect, all in search of a piece of living history and its maker.

Two of these lively kitchens are found in small inns, Casa Luna and La Casa de Espíritus Alegres, where they are used daily in providing sumptuous breakfasts for scores of visiting guests. The others are in private homes, where they delight those cooking at a more relaxed pace. Each kitchen holds a lifetime of memories, but above all, each one reflects a deep respect for and connection with the whimsical and wondrous folk art of Mexico.

above. Massive columns like these are fashioned by stonecutters from *cantera*, a volcanic stone quarried throughout central Mexico. Bright blue and green antique cabinets from the forested state of Michoacán hold a lively collection of painted vases, pots, and glassware.

left. Simple wooden spoons, sold for pennies in the markets of Mexico, become art pieces when displayed against the deep rust-colored walls. Pots below are from the states of Oaxaca, Michoacán, and Guerrero; greenware on the wall hails from Patamban.

page 50. Outdoor dining is a year-round option for guests staying at Casa Luna Bed and Breakfast in San Miguel de Allende. The owner designed this open-air kitchen and dining area as a casual alternative to the more formal indoor options, as well as a place to display her burgeoning folk art collection.

page 51. Vividly hued *aguas frescas* (fresh fruit drinks) capture the flavors of Mexico's multitude of fruits in their cool refreshing liquid. Here, they glow in the sunlight on a table covered with *hule,* the ubiquitous Mexican oilcloth.

left. A tiled roof covers the work area as the afternoon sun casts its long shadows.

below. Banners of *papel picado* (literally, cut paper) decorate Mexico from one end to the other. The majority is now machine-made, but a few artists are still carrying on the tradition of painstakingly cutting it by hand. At Casa Luna, plastic *papel picado* for outdoor use is hung from the rafters, along with brightly painted ceramic cups from Uruapan, Michoacán. Following an old kitchen custom, miniature cups are used to spell out Casa Luna on the wall.

opposite. Ceramics from Michoacán, Guanajuato, and Oaxaca fill the shelves of Casa de Jalatlaco, named for its historic neighborhood in Oaxaca City, and reflect the owners' passion for Mexican pottery. High on the melon-colored wall gleams a cross of hammered tin, a popular craft in Oaxaca City. The modern stove is cobalt blue, a classic Mexican color put to contemporary use.

left, top. A turquoise niche highlights the ceramic collection gathered on travels to many parts of Mexico. The painterly pieces are typical of the work done by Capelo at his studio in the hills above Guanajuato; the large pot is from the pottery town of Dolores Hidalgo. Bluebirds like those on the surrounding tiles are repeated on the walls.

left, bottom. An antique coffee grinder sits below a whimsical tree of life from the village of Ocumicho, Michoacán, where nearly everyone works in clay to create these colorful fantasy pieces.

above. A wild cast of characters — a musical mermaid, embracing chickens, the Virgin of Guadalupe, ceramic market sellers — fills a bright blue shelf with color and whimsy.

left, top. A recessed alcove in blue and turquoise holds *talavera* pottery from Puebla, burnished terra-cotta pots from Michoacán, Oaxacan greenware, and traditional Guanajuato-style glazed pottery.

left, bottom. Striking black masks from Michoacán bedecked with colorful ribbons hang on the wall above three outstanding examples of Mexican ceramic artistry. The *piña* on the left is from San José de Gracia, Michoacán, where numerous artisans have been producing these highly stylized pineapples since the 1930s. A whimsical polychromatic sculpture by Francisco Flores of Izúcar de Matamoros, Puebla, stands in the center. On the right, the *torre* (tower) of stacked green pottery from Patamban, Michoacán, is by Neftalí Ayungua, a well-known ceramicist who learned his craft from his wife some thirty years ago.

opposite. After twenty-five years of collecting, the owners fill every shelf, nook, and niche of their inviting kitchen with their sizable collection of folk art.

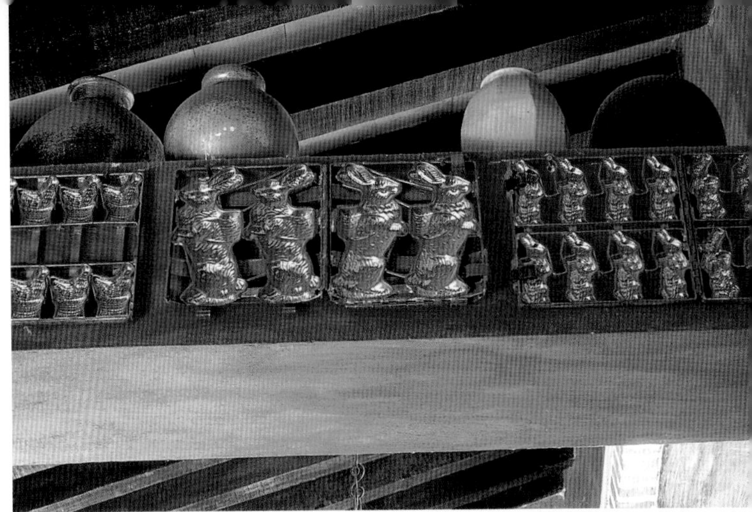

page 59, top. Antique chocolate Easter bunny molds hanging on the beam were brought to Mexico from Hershey, Pennsylvania. Asian-inspired ceramic pots are from Cerámica La Cruz in Valenciana, a village in the hills above Guanajuato.

page 59, bottom. The colorful breakfast area is home to *Napoleon,* a painted wooden statue done by American artist Sandra Berry. *The Rabbit Conspiracy,* crafted by Mario Lopez in the village of Ihuatzio, Michoacán, holds court on the lower right. At Tzimundi, his rural studio, Mario creates furniture and statuary of animal forms by welding together an iron armature that is then covered with woven reeds gathered from the shores of Lake Pátzcuaro.

left. A custom-painted cabinet brightens a corner of the breakfast area and holds an eclectic selection of the owners' American folk art treasures, notably the blown glassware and high-heeled pink sneakers.

page 58. In the Casa de Cinco Perros, Americana met *Mexicana* when the owners melded their lifetime collection of antiques from the eastern United States with their more recently discovered Mexican treasures. When remodeling their kitchen seven years ago, the owners left the original arches above the new stove and workstation but filled them with the unexpected: 1940s neon lights from Alexandria, Virginia. The chrome and Formica dinette set, a 1950s American staple, was a Mexico City estate sale discovery. It is topped with heirloom lace made by the owner's grandmother and a wooden tea set carved by Mario Quiroz, a Tarahumara Indian from Chihuahua. Mario is a carpenter by trade, but his artist's spirit shines through in this whimsical work of art entitled *Ponchera.*

above. In use since pre-Hispanic time, *molcajetes* are lava rock mortars used with a *tejolote*, or pestle, to grind spices, chiles, and other ingredients in Mexican cooking. This charming menagerie, gathered over years of travel to Puebla, Oaxaca, and Guanajuato, reflects the owners' love for animals.

right. A jolly *calaca* (skeleton) works at the desk; shelves are filled with the owners' favorite pieces: a "corncob" of woven vanilla beans from Veracruz, ceramics from Oaxaca and Michoacán, papier-mâché and wooden toys from Celaya, Guanajuato.

opposite, bottom. Cabinet doors and drawer fronts are covered with sheets of hammered tin designed by the owners and executed by a local artisan. The archetype for the glass knobs was found in Sweden and replicated at Guajuye, a glass factory in San Miguel de Allende.

left. El Super Frio lords over the colorful tableau on the fireplace mantel. 1950s monkey bottles from Mitla, Oaxaca, are used to hold mescal, a fermented spirit made from agave. On the right wall, *blanco y negro* plates by the late Natividad Peña are superb examples of the native pottery she originated in Tzintzuntzan, Michoacán. The designs — men fishing, women cooking, children dancing — reflect the simple joys of life on Lake Pátzcuaro.

page 62. Originally constructed in the sixteenth century as part of a silver-mining hacienda, La Casa de Espíritus Alegres was reborn as an artists' retreat in the 1970s, later evolving into a popular bed-and-breakfast. Inspired by the lively spirits found in the art created in Mexico for Día de los Muertos (Day of the Dead), the owners filled their kitchen with skeletons cavorting in every corner. Even the name, the House of the Happy Spirits, comes from the ever-growing collection of smiling skeletons the owners gathered on their trips throughout Mexico.

page 63, top. An abundance of fresh fruit and cheery oilcloth add to the happy mood at La Casa de Espíritus Alegres. The colorful equestrians in line above the range were made by local papier-mâché-craftswoman Juana Andrade, whom the owner discovered selling her wares on the streets of Guanajuato during the Easter market. The vividly colored pottery pieces are from the pottery town of Dolores Hidalgo, just a half hour's ride away.

Avocado Dip with Seasonal Fruit

Guacamole Chamacuero

INGREDIENTS

Serves 6

- ½ small white onion, chopped (about 2 heaping tablespoons)
- 2 to 3 serrano chiles, finely chopped
- ½ teaspoon salt, or to taste
- 2 ripe avocados
- 1 ripe peach, peeled, pitted, and finely diced
- ½ cup halved seedless grapes
- 1½ tablespoons fresh lime juice (about one lime), or to taste
- ⅓ cup pomegranate seeds
- Tortilla chips for dipping

This chunky avocado dip with chopped fresh fruit sounds completely contemporary, but it is a time-honored recipe from the town of Comonfort, Guanajuato, published by Diana Kennedy in her excellent cookbook/travel memoir, *My Mexico.* Chamacuero is the indigenous name for Comonfort, where this recipe is made in the late summer and fall when the pomegranates are bursting with ruby-red seeds. The juicy crunch of the grapes and the pomegranate seeds adds a surprising textural layer to the smooth richness of the savory avocado mixture, and, as a garnish, the seeds float like sparkling garnets on a sea of green.

If you own one, use your *molcajete y tejolote* (lava-rock mortar and pestle) to make this recipe in the traditional manner.

1 In a *molcajete*, or on a cutting board with a knife, crush the onion, chiles, and salt together to a paste. Remove the pit and peel from the avocados, and roughly crush the pulp with your hands into the *molcajete*, or put the onion-chile mixture in a mixing bowl and add the pulp to the bowl, stirring to combine.

2 Add the peach, grapes, lime juice, and about half of the pomegranate seeds. Mix well, adding more salt or lime to taste.

3 Serve in the *molcajete*, or transfer to a serving bowl, and sprinkle with the remaining pomegranate seeds. Pass the tortilla chips.

chapter 5

Eternal Springtime

Classic Cuernavaca kitchens at Casa de la Torre and Casa Ahuilayan

RECIPE: BRIE QUESADILLAS WITH FRESH FRUIT SALSA, QUESADILLAS DE BRIE CON SALSA DE FRUTA

Known as the "City of Eternal Springtime," Cuernavaca is rightfully famous for its abundant gardens and pleasant year-round climate. At Casa de la Torre and Casa Ahuilayan, the feeling of spring extends into lushly tiled kitchens that glow with sunlight. The similarity of these two kitchens is no accident; when the homes were remodeled in the 1960s, the fellow expatriate owners compared notes and shared design ideas. At Casa Ahuilayan, Donal Cordry, a self-taught Mesoamerican scholar and author of several books on Mexican crafts, built a sweeping archway covered with tiles in classic *talavera* yellow and blue to delineate the two workspaces of his kitchen. Robert Brady, an American artist and designer who had recently purchased Casa de la Torre, employed a similar expansive arch and cheerful colors in his kitchen as well, this time adding an unexpected orange to the palette.

Donal and Robert left behind two delightful examples of modern kitchens designed with a traditional Mexican sensibility. Casa de la Torre, tucked behind Cuernavaca's cathedral in a sixteenth-century building that once housed a Franciscan monastery, is now open to the public as the Robert Brady Museum. With his inimitable artist's eye, Brady stylishly filled his home with a diverse collection of art, furniture, and artifacts from around the world, and the kitchen is just one of fourteen remarkable rooms visitors may see, each as fabulous as the next. Casa Ahuilayan, which translates to "house of enchantment and joy" in Nahuatl, remains a private home, the gracious owner's enchanted and joyful sanctuary from the hustle of modern Cuernavaca just outside the bougainvillea-covered walls.

top. Tucked into a niche where the tiled column and archway meet is a collection of shiny brass and copper coffeepots from Mexico, Turkey, and India.

above. The ubiquitous bluebirds on these kitchen tiles — flying upward for good luck — are similar in style to Delftware from the Netherlands, evidence of the European influence in Mexican *talavera.*

opposite. Next to the modern range in the kitchen of Casa de la Torre is an old-style stovetop decked out in blue-and-white tiles of various classic *talavera* designs.

page 66. In the kitchen of Casa de la Torre, the stovetops — one traditional, one modern — are located in a recessed alcove filled with sunshine from the skylight above. Garlands of garlic cloves are strung above the stove, a Mexican good luck talisman.

page 67. In this tile painting of San Pasqual Bailón, patron saint of cooks and kitchens, the ever-pious monk is seen kneeling before his hearth surrounded by the accoutrements of a busy kitchen and his loyal cat.

above. His beloved cook, Maria, still oversees the kitchen of Casa de la Torre in this vivid portrait done by Brady. Through the arched doorway, we catch a glimpse of the formal dining room and the open-air living room beyond.

left. A *talavera* tea set from Puebla fills the shelf between the tiled arch and column.

opposite, left. A gourd soup tureen with sterling silver trim and ladle is an unexpected combination of the natural and manmade. Gourds are hollowed and dried before the silver handles, lid, and monogram are fashioned to fit. The plate is from Tonalá, a pottery-producing town just outside Guadalajara.

opposite, right. Beams, floor, and furniture are boldly painted brilliant orange to match the Moorish patterned tiles; miniature baking dishes festoon the wall above.

left. Tiles from nearby Puebla are the defining feature of the kitchen at Casa Ahuilayan, where they cover the walls, ceiling, shelves, counters, and hood over the stove. Broad swaths of solid color are interspersed with various geometric patterns in a delightful feast for the eyes.

opposite, left. Arches abound, drawing the visitor's eye to the dining room and garden beyond. The painting of pears is by Alicia Blumenkron. Tiled shelves on the left hold canisters from Cerámica Amora in Dolores Hidalgo and the owner's favorite cookbooks.

opposite, right. A yellow tiled wall serves as a partition between the dining room and the work area of the kitchen, as well as providing the ideal spot for a tile mural of classic Puebla design. The formal silver tea set, still in use today, was purchased in the 1940s at Sanborn's, once upon a time the Tiffany's of Mexico.

left. Though plumbed for gas, the curved tile-covered cooktop is modeled after the wood-burning stoves of old Mexico. Firewood was stored in the arched area below, now home to a *metate y mano,* a stone grinding surface and rolling pin.

below. Lines of grout create a geometric puzzle in the uniquely curved corner stove-top. The covered *casuelas* (cooking dishes), once properly seasoned, go from stovetop to oven and are used to prepare rice, stews, beans, and sauces.

above. A trip to the *mercado* (market) in any Mexican town yields a bounty of vegetables such as these found bathed in sunlight at Casa Ahuilayan.

Brie Quesadillas with Fresh Fruit Salsa

Quesadillas de Brie con Salsa de Fruta

The classic quesadilla of Mexico is updated here with Brie cheese and sweetened nuts, and served as an appetizer with a bright and tangy salsa of fresh mango and pineapple. This salsa is also wonderful served on grilled chicken or fish.

It is important to chop all the salsa ingredients the same size—about ½-inch square—so that each bite will have the right balance of flavors. Ingredients for the salsa may be prepped ahead, but don't mix them together more than an hour before serving, or the acid in the pineapple will soften the delicate mango.

The recipe for Candied Walnuts will make more than you need, but the extras are great to have on hand to sprinkle on salads and desserts.

INGREDIENTS

Serves 6

1 POUND BRIE CHEESE, WELL CHILLED

TWELVE 5- OR 6-INCH FLOUR TORTILLAS

1 SMALL BUNCH CILANTRO, LARGE STEMS REMOVED

½ CUP CANDIED WALNUTS, *recipe follows*

NONSTICK COOKING SPRAY

1½ CUPS FRESH FRUIT SALSA, *recipe follows*

Candied Walnuts

Makes about 1 cup

1 CUP WALNUT PIECES

2 TABLESPOONS MAPLE SYRUP

Fresh Fruit Salsa

Makes about 1½ cups

½ CUP DICED PINEAPPLE

½ CUP DICED MANGO (ABOUT 1 MEDIUM MANGO)

¼ CUP DICED RED BELL PEPPER (ABOUT ¼ PEPPER)

2 TABLESPOONS CILANTRO, CHOPPED

½ SERRANO CHILE, MINCED

1 TEASPOON SUGAR, OR TO TASTE

2 TEASPOONS RICE WINE VINEGAR, SEASONED OR PLAIN, OR TO TASTE

JUICE OF ONE LIME

SPRINKLE OF SALT, OR TO TASTE

1 **Cut the rind off the sides of the Brie and cut it into ½-inch-thick slices.** Lay 6 of the tortillas out on a clean work surface. Divide the Brie and Candied Walnuts evenly among the tortillas and place 4 to 6 sprigs of cilantro on each. Place the remaining tortillas on top to enclose the filling. Chill, wrapped in plastic wrap, for at least 1 hour and up to 8 hours.

2 **Heat a flat griddle over medium-high heat.** Spray the griddle lightly with nonstick cooking spray and cook the quesadillas, turning once, until they are slightly browned, about 5 minutes. Place them on a cutting board and allow them to set up for a minute or two before cutting each into 8 wedges. Serve with Fresh Fruit Salsa.

Candied Walnuts

In a bowl, toss the walnuts with the maple syrup to coat. Place the walnuts on a foil-lined sheet and bake them at 300°F for 20 to 25 minutes, stirring several times, until they are lightly browned and the syrup has reduced to a glaze. Allow them to cool slightly, then remove them from the foil and store them in an airtight container until ready to serve, or for up to 2 weeks.

Fresh Fruit Salsa

In a nonreactive mixing bowl, gently mix all salsa ingredients. Check the seasoning, adding sugar, vinegar, or salt to taste. Chill for no more than 1 hour and serve with Brie Quesadillas.

chapter 6

Ablaze with Color

The richly hued kitchens of Casa Chuparosa, El Refugio, Casa Reyes-Larraín, and Casa del Pocito

RECIPE: SALAD OF BABY GREENS WITH ROASTED BEETS, AVOCADO, AND FRESH CHEESE, ENSALADA VERDE CON BETABEL, AGUACATE, Y QUESO FRESCO

Mexico, it seems, has always been in love with color. Pre-Columbian Mexico was a polychromatic world, its edifices and frescoes painted in deep blues and greens, blends of red and yellow, black and white. Throughout history, Mexico's painters, weavers, and artisans have used pigments from the world around them—minerals, vegetables, insects, and seashells—to create warm ochre yellow, lustrous indigo blue, radiant carmine red, and the palest of purples.

Modern Mexico continues to glow with bold, true colors. One look at the crazy quilt of houses tumbling down a hillside in Guanajuato, a Mayan *huipil* (tunic) in Chiapas embroidered in the brilliant hues of a tropical bird, or the multicolored rug hanging on a line in a dusty village in Oaxaca and it is clear that Mexico truly is, as author Elena Poniatowska wrote, "a resting place for the rainbow."

When restoring their colonial-era home in San Miguel de Allende, the owners of Casa Chuparosa chose deep burnished red and warm cream to color their kitchen, hues they found in the glazes of eighteenth-century tiles rescued from the original home. In the lakeside town of Pátzcuaro, where each tile-roofed house lining every cobblestoned street is painted identically—whitewashed upper walls with a brick red wainscot—the owner's unique style emerged on kitchen walls washed with colors found in his favorite paintings. And in Mérida, the capital city of Yucatán, the architect-design team of Salvador Reyes-Ríos and Josefina Larraín coaxed the sun and sky indoors, using vivid yellows and blues to brighten two of their distinctively designed kitchens.

above. A string of garlic for good luck hangs from an antique wooden *trastero* (shelf for dishes) holding a collection of decorative — and useful — ceramic plates and platters.

left, top. The original stone sink remains, now encased in poured concrete tinted the same burnished red as the walls. Tile edging and accents provide visual interest and continuity.

left, bottom. Antique *talavera* tiles from the original kitchen form a decorative montage on the wall. *Equipal* stools are conveniently placed near an antique table by the stove. *Equipal,* from the Nahuatl word for seat, is a popular style of Mexican furniture made from wood, palm, and pigskin dating back to the time of Aztec rule.

left. Masterfully carved wooden drawer fronts were custom-made by talented carpenters in San Miguel. A simple vignette of glowing green limes and a cobalt-blue *olla* (cooking pot) provide visual allure on the counter above.

bottom, left. Gleaming copper pots from Santa Clara del Cobre hang on wrought-iron hooks from the mesquite beam above the stove.

bottom, right. With a stroke of brilliance, the owners retained the colonial ambience of their up-to-date kitchen by placing the modern appliances behind these massive mesquite doors. A forged iron chandelier hangs from the whitewashed ceiling inset with skylights.

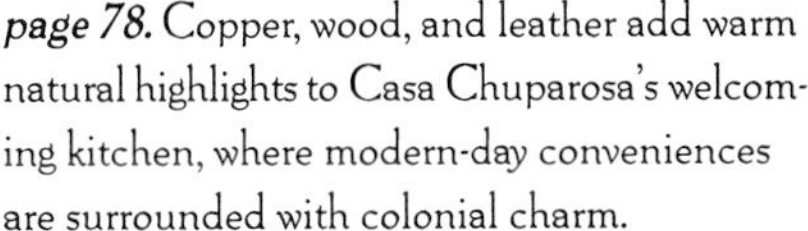

page 78. Copper, wood, and leather add warm natural highlights to Casa Chuparosa's welcoming kitchen, where modern-day conveniences are surrounded with colonial charm.

page 79. The bounty of Mexico's orchards and farms fills a distinctive rectangular ceramic tray with color.

below. Inside the doors of El Refugio, a pleasant refuge for travelers tucked behind Pátzcuaro's basilica, the kitchen walls glow in lemon yellow and melon orange.

opposite, top left. Miniature clay cups from Uruapan and a bright-blue stripe outline the wainscot and cabinetry in the comfortable kitchen of El Refugio. A *torre* (tower) of glazed greenware from nearby Patambam and a giant *casuela* (cooking dish) lean against the wall.

opposite, top right. Hand-painted floral motifs were added above the archway leading to the dining room. A playful painting by Soledad hangs on the wall. (If you look very closely, you can see a portrait of the owner just above the watermelon.) The vivid colors in this work inspired the shades used on the kitchen walls.

opposite, bottom. Wooden spoons become art when displayed on this decorative holder in the traditional chip-carved style of Michoacán.

top. A simple iron bar placed above polished concrete countertops provides a home for pots and pans. The distinctive bas-relief pattern along the edge of the *campana*, its design inspired by French floor tiles common in Mérida, was stamped into the fresh cement with a wooden mold.

above. Tiles old and new are arranged in a relaxed mosaic on the counter front.

left. Henequen, a fiber harvested from the agave plant used for making cord and rope, was once the "green gold" crop of the Yucatán Peninsula. Here woven reminders of that illustrious past adorn the wall.

opposite. Reyes-Larraín kitchens feature classic colonial bones with a sleek updated look, a trademark of this innovative couple. In their own home, the architect-designers took the traditional *campana* (hood) over the stove and expanded its width to match the scale of the room. This oversized *campana* has become all-but synonymous with work of this talented team. The colors of the kitchen fairly sing; azure blue glows against golden apricot walls. Red and white geometric cement floor tiles are the originals, the color echoed on the door.

below. Cerulean blue walls and luminous yellow tiles bring light and life to the kitchen of Casa del Pocito. Arches under the hearth were a common feature in colonial Mexican kitchens; here they have been exaggerated, providing architectural interest as well as practical storage below the work counter.

opposite, top left. Set into the red concrete countertop, the sink was lined with tiles recycled from the original house, a subtle reminder of the past.

opposite, top right. Earthenware dishes for cooking, *casuelas* in Spanish, hang from the shelf above the workspace, where they are readily available.

opposite, bottom left. The eight-pointed star, here in a quilt-like rendering of solids and florals, is a common *talavera* tile pattern with Persian roots.

opposite, bottom right. Against a washed blue wall, blood-red gladiolas and bright yellow tiles complete the trinity of primary colors. The turnip painting by Hattie Kronsberg, in the same three tones, heightens the drama.

above. A modern stovetop, set into an equally modern concrete counter, is balanced by the colonial-style wooden brackets of the shelf where traditional earthenware *casuelas* (cooking dishes) hang.

Salad of Baby Greens with Roasted Beets, Avocado, and Fresh Cheese

Ensalada Verde con Betabel, Aguacate, y Queso Fresco

INGREDIENTS

Serves 8

4 MEDIUM BEETS

2 TABLESPOONS BALSAMIC VINEGAR

SALT AND FRESHLY GROUND PEPPER TO TASTE

2 RIPE AVOCADOS

1 POUND MIXED BABY GREENS

CITRUS VINAIGRETTE, *recipe follows*

4 OUNCES QUESO FRESCO, CRUMBLED

Citrus Vinaigrette

Makes about ¾ cup

½ CUP FRESH ORANGE JUICE

1 TABLESPOON FRESH LIME JUICE

¼ CUP OLIVE OIL

1 SHALLOT CLOVE, MINCED

SALT AND FRESHLY GROUND PEPPER TO TASTE

Garnet-red beets, jade-green avocado, and pearly-white cheese make this salad as pleasing to the eye as it is to the palate. The beets are cut and peeled before cooking so that their natural sweetness is heightened when roasted with a sprinkle of balsamic vinegar. Haas avocados, with their buttery rich flesh, are the ones to use for this salad. *Queso fresco,* literally "fresh cheese," is a staple of Mexican cooking and is made in rural homes throughout Mexico. A pasteurized version is available in Mexican markets and many large supermarkets. If you can't find it, feta cheese is a flavorful, if not traditional, substitute.

For the best presentation, toss the greens with the vinaigrette, then place them in the serving bowl or on salad plates before you arrange the vegetables and cheese on top.

1 **Preheat the oven to 350°F.**

2 **Using a sharp paring knife, peel the beets and cut into wedges.** In a medium bowl, toss the beets with the balsamic vinegar and place on a sheet of heavy-duty foil on a sheet pan. Season with salt and pepper. Top with another sheet of foil and crimp the edges to seal. Roast the beets for about 30 minutes, until tender. Let them cool in the foil.

3 **Slice the avocados.**

4 **Toss the greens with the vinaigrette to taste** and place them in a serving bowl or on individual salad plates. Arrange the avocado slices and beet wedges on top of the greens. Sprinkle with the cheese.

Citrus Vinaigrette

In a nonreactive mixing bowl, whisk all the vinaigrette ingredients together until well blended.

The vinaigrette may be made ahead and stored in the refrigerator for up to 2 days.

Miles of Tiles

Exquisite tile work adorns the kitchens of Susurro, Casa de Vino Tinto, Villa el Cerrito, and Quinta Quebrada

RECIPE: CHILLED MANGO SOUP, GAZPACHO DE MANGO

Consider the beauty of one individually handcrafted glazed tile—a work of art in its own right. Multiply that singular beauty by the thousands of individual tiles in an average kitchen, add a multitude of glaze colors and hand-painted designs, amplify it with innumerable pattern combinations, and you're looking at an unending world of possibilities.

Though primitive tiled surfaces are known to have existed far back as 4700 B.C., the art of making decorative tile was perfected in Spain during seven hundred years of Moorish occupation. (Even the Spanish word for tile, *azulejo*, is a derivative of the Arabic word for "little glazed stone.") From the tenth to the sixteenth centuries, the Islamic impact on Spain was profound on many fronts, but nowhere was the influence more strikingly visible than in the colors, the designs, and the lavish abundance of tiles that covered the palaces, churches, mosques, and homes of Spain. After the Reconquest of Spain, a broader range of glaze colors for the tiles came from Italy and France, and porcelain designs from the Far East added flora and fauna motifs; though the original Moorish colors and geometric designs remain popular to this day.

In the sixteenth century, the Spanish introduced this highly decorative art to Mexico, when potters from Talavera de la Reina, Spain, brought their tin-glazed earthenware to the city of Puebla. The indigenous influence was added to the mix, and *talavera* pottery was born in Nueva España. The potters set to work making ceramic dinnerware, utilitarian pottery, and tiles with which to cover the churches and cathedrals of the New World. Puebla became a tile-coated city, and in the prosperous towns along the Silver Route—and eventually throughout the country—tiles covered the fountains, facades, domes, floors, and walls of Mexico.

Tiles continue to adorn and enhance the homes of Mexico with their timeless beauty, as illustrated in the four glorious tile masterpieces featured here.

above. Pale-pink carved *cantera* buttresses support the massive beam running the length of the kitchen. *Cantera,* a volcanic stone, is found in varying shades of pink, beige, and green throughout central Mexico.

left, top. Calla lilies glow in a sunlit corner of the Susurro kitchen. White tile countertops and a creamy blue wall set off the still life tile panel. Atop the massive beam are copper pots from Santa Clara del Cobre; the large, bold charger is the work of the owner, a ceramic artist himself.

left, bottom. Freshly baked bread, a basket of fruit, and an *olla* (cooking pot) filled with wooden utensils bask in the morning sunlight pouring through the deeply recessed kitchen window.

opposite. From the stained herringbone-pattern brick floor to the massive wooden ceiling beams, the kitchen was lovingly rebuilt with respect for the home's colonial heritage. The design of the tile mural is the work of the owner, who drew on antique Portuguese tiles and photographs of old Mexican kitchens when he created this tour de force. He took his ideas to Uriarte, the oldest *talavera* studio in Puebla, to have his vision transformed into tile.

page 90. Purchased in ruins in 2001 and subjected to fourteen months of teardown and reconstruction, Susurro Bed and Breakfast in San Miguel de Allende now offers guests a peaceful haven within its walls. The true masterpiece of the kitchen is the exquisite tile mural that runs the length of the room. The style is pure Renaissance, inspired by the owner's sojourns in France, Portugal, and Italy.

page 91. Painting these tiles required a master, and the decades of experience of the venerable Uriarte *talavera* studio are evident in each perfectly placed brushstroke. Tile-setters in Mexico are artists in their own right, skilled at tightly fitting hundreds of tiles with perfect precision.

PERFECT
P
COFFEE

above. Three colorful ceramic fruit sellers by the Aguilar family in Ocotlán, Oaxaca, stand atop the fire-engine red and caution yellow spice shelf.

left. Boldly colored tiles from Dolores Hidalgo over the stove provide an exciting focal point in the brilliant yellow kitchen of Casa de Vino Tinto in Oaxaca. Ground metal oxides create the intense yellow glaze of the edging tiles.

opposite, left. The arrangement of these jewel-toned tiles creates a repeating "wallpaper pattern," which is clearly illustrated on the wall and hood of the stove.

opposite, right. Islamic law disallowed painted figures of humans and animals, so tile patterns like these were developed, revealing the mathematically focused minds of their designers. Red grouting heightens the geometric effect.

left. The glazes of the *piña* (pineapple) from Michoacán on the counter and the *azulejos* (tiles) from Dolores Hidalgo contain the same mineral pigments, as their harmonious yellows and greens demonstrate.

below. The intricately painted kitchen table and chairs were crafted in a highland village in Guatemala, where the owner once lived and worked.

opposite. The subtle two-tone palette in the kitchen of Villa el Cerrito in San Miguel de Allende is elegant in its simplicity. Deep-blue patterned tiles outline the doorways and arches, while solid cream tiles cover the walls and domed ceiling. Under an ornate iron chandelier forged by a local blacksmith, a tile-wrapped center island provides a convenient workspace as well as storage. The whimsical ceramic animals are by Gorky Gonzales of nearby Guananjuato.

left, top. Single-motif tiles like these surrounding the recessed shelves are complete unto themselves, requiring no other tiles to produce a pattern. The deep-blue dishes on the middle shelves are painted in the classic pointillist design of Capula, Michoacán, where they are now being produced with food-safe glazes, thanks to the work of Barro Sin Plomo (Clay without Lead), an organization dedicated to developing lead-free glazes that retain the quality and colors of the past.

left, bottom. *Bóvedas,* the vaulted brick ceilings of Mexico, are a wonder to behold. While their beauty is unquestionable in the finished state, the process of building one is a work of art as well. Without any underlying framework, a *bovedero* lays moistened bricks in place, beginning at the corners and working inward and upward, round and round the room until the last brick is laid in place. *Bóvedas* are often left unadorned, but the opulent veneer of cream tiles at Villa el Cerrito only enhances its beauty with yet another layer of craftsmanship.

right, top. These ceramic pieces are exceptional examples from the Guanajuato studios of Gorky Gonzales and Capelo, two talented masters. While a broad range of glaze colors is now available to potters, this simple cobalt-and-white palette, a favorite of both the Moors and the Chinese, remains popular today.

right, bottom. An antique wooden bowl from Morocco holds decorative green glazed spheres from the pottery studios of Patamban, Michoacán. Painted wooden trays like those adorning the wall are still made in Michoacán; these were gleaned from antiques stores in San Miguel.

opposite. In the breakfast room area just off the kitchen, the owner wanted to "have fun." In contrast to the formality of her cream-tiled kitchen, here she painted the stucco walls and built-in cabinetry a soft spring green to complement the painted wooden cabinet.

EL PAN NUESTRO DE CADA DIA

above. In this lavishly tiled corner of the kitchen, the numerous geometric patterns in the tile-wrapped bench, wainscoting, and trim are visually harmonious, owing to the use of a simple two-color palette.

left, middle. Moorish and Chinese influences are evident in the colors, motifs, and shapes in this collection of *talavera* vases and pots found atop the tiled walls of Quinta Quebrada.

left, bottom. A sea of cobalt-and-cream *talavera* tiles cleverly encloses the appliances and covers the countertops and stove. Ceramic canisters from various pottery studios in Dolores Hidalgo hold flour, sugar, and other staples at the ready.

opposite. Copper pots from Michoacán hang from the rafters in Quinta Quebrada in San Miguel de Allende. In an unusual twist, the ubiquitous bluebirds on the tiles all but disappear into the geometric pattern formed when a quartet of tiles is placed facing the center. Animal-themed pottery on the wall is typical of the Guanajuato style; these are by Gorky Gonzales.

above. Decades of use are evident in the well-worn surfaces of these copper kettles from Santa Clara del Cobre, Michoacán. Copper has been worked in Santa Clara since pre-Hispanic times, but production of these two-handled pots (*cazos*) began in the sixteenth century by order of Bishop Vasco de Quiroga, a benevolent Franciscan friar who believed that the production of a saleable craft was the key to autonomy for the indigenous people of Michoacán. Coppersmiths working in Santa Clara today still use pre-Hispanic methods — smelting with a bellows without a crucible and forging on stone — as they continue to realize Quiroga's vision.

Chilled Mango Soup

Gazpacho de Mango

INGREDIENTS

※※※ **Serves 6** ※※※

3 ripe mangoes, peeled and pitted (or about 1½ cups of frozen mango)

1 tablespoon brown sugar, firmly packed

2 tablespoons vegetable oil (not olive oil; it is too strongly flavored)

¼ cup rice wine vinegar, seasoned or plain

1 cup water

1 teaspoon minced fresh ginger root

½ teaspoon salt, or to taste

¼ teaspoon white pepper

1 ripe mango, peeled, pitted, and finely chopped

1 medium cucumber, peeled, seeded, and finely chopped (or ½ English cucumber)

½ small red onion, peeled and finely chopped

2 tablespoons chopped chives for garnish (optional)

The mango, now so common in Mexican cuisine, was an immigrant to Mexico, transported from the Far East in galleons laden with exotic flavors such as cinnamon, ginger, and cloves. It adapted to its new home with gusto; Mexico is now the largest mango exporter in the world.

Mangoes are at their peak during the summer months, when you'll be able to choose from many different types, but I've made this soup even in the winter with frozen mango chunks, and it was still delicious. You can always adjust for sweetness or tartness by adding a bit more sugar or vinegar.

This recipe comes from Martha Hyder, a remarkable and charming Texan, and the doyenne of the venerable Quinta Quebrada in San Miguel de Allende.

※ ※ ※ ※ ※

1 In two batches, puree the mango pulp in a blender with the brown sugar, oil, rice wine vinegar, and water until smooth. Add the ginger, salt, and pepper and blend. Add more water if needed to achieve the consistency you prefer. Add more salt if you like. Transfer to a large bowl. Reserving 2 tablespoons of each for garnish, stir the chopped mango, cucumber, and red onion into the soup. Cover and chill for at least 2 hours or overnight (also cover and chill the garnishes).

2 To serve, pour the soup into chilled serving bowls or cups, and sprinkle garnishes on top.

chapter 8

Treasured Collections

Antiques fill the kitchens of Casa Holler-Saunders and La Quinta de San Antonio

RECIPE: PORK AND HOMINY STEW WITH TOMATILLOS, POZOLE VERDE

One of the most remarkable things about grand Mexican homes is that their majesty is so often hidden behind looming stone and stucco walls. Passersby are given no hint of the splendor just behind the gates. But splendor there is, as these two Spanish colonial–period homes illustrate. Both homes, one located in Morelia and the other in Puebla, two of Mexico's most beautiful colonial cities, are owned by antiques dealers and home designers, and their distinctive styles spill from their sophisticated living spaces into their glorious kitchens.

Noting the need for a "civilized" European city to replace indigenous-run Pátzcuaro, New Spain's first viceroy, Antonio de Mendoza, founded Morelia in 1542. The city was well planned, with wide streets and large plazas laid out in an orderly grid. The pink stone buildings in Morelia's *centro histórico* (historic central district) remain some of Mexico's finest examples of Spanish colonial architecture, and the magnificent mansions now house museums, government offices, banks, and private residences. Casa Holler-Saunders, behind its high stucco walls, is one such home. While the busy capital city rumbles by outside, the owners' civilized enclave—and the kitchen they designed—reflects their respect for Morelia's noble past as well as their appreciation of contemporary style.

Puebla has long served as Mexico's treasure chest. One of the first cities founded by Hernán Cortez upon his arrival in New Spain, Puebla was advantageously located midway between Mexico City and the ports of Veracruz and Acapulco, first in line for the wealth of resources arriving from Europe and the Far East, and the last stop for the riches of Mexico's prolific mines bound for Spain. The opulent residences and well-financed convents of Puebla boasted fine porcelain from France and China; silks and spices from the Far East; Italian, English, and French furniture inlaid with mother-of-pearl, ivory, and silver; and the finest examples of Puebla's own *talavera* pottery. The stately homes of today's Puebla offer a glimpse of this grandeur, as La Quinta de San Antonio illustrates. Filled to overflowing with inherited and discovered treasures, the kitchen in this former convent expresses the owners' deep connection to Puebla's distinguished history.

above. Ceramic water jars from the state of Guerrero share space with humorous statuettes known as *los borrachos* (the drunks). Popular in the 1950s, statues such as these poked fun at popular politicos.

left. The fresco in a sixteenth-century monastery in nearby Cuitzeo provided the fascinating design — strict geometrics with a florid border — that was meticulously replicated throughout the kitchen.

opposite. The splashes of blue found in an antique *talavera* bowl from Puebla, a Moorish-inspired zigzag-striped ginger jar from Dolores Hidalgo, antique statuettes on the shelves, and a swath of light above the refrigerator tie together the eclectic collection in the kitchen of Casa Holler-Saunders with their brilliant azure hue.

page 106. Shadow and light, old and new, formal and casual, industrial and natural — contrast sets a dramatic tone in the kitchen of Casa Holler-Saunders, a renovated sixteenth-century colonial home in Morelia. Matte-finished deep terra-cotta walls are set off by the lustrous stainless-steel hood and a dazzling oil painting.

page 107. On the wooden countertop, humorous smiling portraits adorn ceramic jugs for *pulque* (a fermented drink made from agave), their heads bursting with fresh blooms.

above. A dreamlike tableau in the stone-walled patio mixes contemporary with classic: an oversized silver-plated chandelier by Holler and Saunders, Ltd., hangs above a simple wrought-iron breakfast table set with silver goblets and a ceramic layer cake.

left. The stone basin in the courtyard dates back to 1598, when it was used for washing dishes. Today it is surrounded by an artistic grouping of stone statuary, creating a restful fountain area.

opposite. Mesquite doors and antique artworks line the wall alongside the thoroughly modern stainless-steel hood and stools.

right. A frosted-glass chandelier in the neoclassic style popular in Puebla in the late 1800s illuminates the kitchen of La Quinta de San Antonio. An animal motif tablecloth embroidered in brilliant yellow is from the Otomí village of San Pablito Pahuatlán, Puebla.

opposite, top. The range of glaze colors used in *talavera* has expanded over the years to include the extensive array of colors shown in these exquisite examples of contemporary tiles fronting the sink. The muted-color tiles around the niche are antiques that were gleaned from the original kitchen.

opposite, bottom left. Wooden spoons, spatulas, and *molinillos* (carved whisks used for frothing hot chocolate) are stored in racks. Multicolored tiles form a decorative cross on the back wall. Note the 1950s yellow-and-white pitcher from Taxco on the counter, an estate sale find that perfectly matches the embroidered Otomí tablecloth in La Quinta de San Antonio's kitchen.

opposite, bottom right. In a tiled niche, nineteenth-century fine white china (*loza fina*) from Puebla, porcelain tureens from France, and blue-trimmed plates from Holland are displayed on rustic shelves of *sabino*, a local cypress.

above. A terra-cotta Virgin of Guadalupe and filigreed candlesticks rest on a shelf of *cantera,* a locally quarried volcanic stone. Dried herbs and flowers hang decoratively from the beam.

right. A footed *talavera* fruit dish and plate, a contemporary piece in classic blue and white, catches the afternoon sun atop a golden-yellow embroidered tablecloth.

opposite, top. Old tiles from the original kitchen provide an interesting background to a mix of heirlooms, antiques, and kitchen utensils. The German-styled oak clock from the Ansonia Clock Company of New York was a very popular item in 1920s Puebla; this one was the prized possession of the owner's grandmother. On the left, a carved wooden tortilla marker, used to decoratively mark tortillas for special occasions, now serves as a trivet.

opposite, bottom left. Heirloom china is stored behind the glass doors of this wooden cabinet.

opposite, bottom right. A massive wooden *trastero* (shelf for dishes) holds cookbooks and mementos as well as a collection of eighteenth-and-nineteenth century *pozoleros*— deep bowls in which pozole, a hominy stew, is traditionally served.

Pork and Hominy Stew with Tomatillos

Pozole Verde

INGREDIENTS

Serves 8

2 POUNDS PORK SHOULDER, TRIMMED OF FAT AND CUT INTO 1-INCH CUBES

2½ TEASPOONS SALT

3 CLOVES GARLIC, PEELED

2 ONIONS, WHITE OR YELLOW, PEELED AND CHOPPED

1 TEASPOON DRIED OREGANO

ABOUT 2 QUARTS PLUS 1 CUP WATER

2 POUNDS TOMATILLOS, HUSKS REMOVED

1 BUNCH FRESH CILANTRO (ABOUT 2 CUPS LOOSELY PACKED)

1 TO 2 SERRANO CHILES

1 POUND FRESH HOMINY OR TWO 29-OUNCE CANS, DRAINED

Accompaniments

½ HEAD GREEN CABBAGE, SHREDDED

6 LIMES, CUT INTO WEDGES

12 RADISHES, SLICED

1 SMALL WHITE ONION, CHOPPED

2 TABLESPOONS DRIED OREGANO

12 TOSTADAS

MEXICAN HOT SAUCE TO TASTE

A flavorful hominy stew is prepared differently depending on the region of Mexico; in Jalisco and Puebla, residents love *pozole blanco* with a natural broth; in Michoacán, *pozole rojo* is made using guajillo and ancho chiles; a traditional recipe from Guerrero calls for wild sorrel and ground pumpkin seed; and along the coasts it is often made with fresh and dried shrimp. This recipe is inspired by two *pozoles* I enjoyed, one in a fabulous little family restaurant on the side of the highway in Guanajuato, and one made by my friend Mima, who hails from Nayarit. I don't know how authentic this *pozole* is, but I do know that it's the best I've ever eaten. As is the case with all stews like this one, the flavor is *much* better if you make it a day before you plan to serve it.

If you can find fresh hominy in the refrigerated section of the market, by all means use it, but if not, canned hominy (also often called *pozole*) will do.

Don't forget that your *pozole* is not truly finished until diners season it to their liking with the traditional accompaniments; they're not just garnish, they're part of the dish.

1 **Place the pork in a heavy 3- or 4-quart pot** with 2 teaspoons of the salt, the garlic, onions, and oregano. Add 2 quarts of the water (add more if needed to cover). Bring to a boil over medium heat and remove any foam that forms on top. Cover, reduce heat to low, and simmer for about 1½ hours, until the meat is almost tender. Remove from heat.

2 **Cook the tomatillos in the 1 cup of water** and the remaining ½ teaspoon of salt in a covered saucepan over low heat for 10 to 15 minutes. They will be softened and no longer bright green. Remove from heat and let them cool.

3 **In a blender, place about 2 cups of cooked tomatillos,** a handful of cilantro, half a serrano chile, and 1 cup of broth from the meat, and puree. Pour this puree into the pot of meat. Repeat until you've pureed all the tomatillos, chiles, and cilantro. Add the hominy to the pot, stir to combine, and simmer over low heat for 30 minutes. The pork will be meltingly tender, and the hominy will open up into "flowers." Allow to cool, then chill overnight.

4 **To serve, bring the *pozole* back to a boil over medium-high heat.** Lower the heat and allow to simmer until the meat is heated through. Transfer piping hot to deep bowls filled about halfway, leaving room for all the accompaniments to be piled on top.

opposite. Above the tiled counter, a massive pine beam holds a stone shelf lined with treasures from the owners' antiques shop. San Antonio, the home's namesake saint, watches from on high.

chapter 9

Traditions of Excellence

Ceramics on display in the kitchens of Casa de Hypatia, Casa Ramos, Casa Encantada, and Casa Estrella

RECIPE: BONELESS CHICKEN BREAST WITH ORANGE-CHIPOTLE SAUCE,
PECHUGA DE POLLO CON SALSA DE NARANJA CON CHIPOTLE

Mexico's deep connection with products made of clay—both decorative and utilitarian—reaches back thousands of years, to pieces created for ceremonial use as well as the earthenware cooking pots of Mexico, *ollas* and *casuelas,* and the *comal de barro,* a flat clay disc on which tortillas were cooked and vegetables were roasted. The age-old design of this Mexican clay kitchenware remains relatively unchanged, their beauty found in the utter simplicity and quirky individuality of each handmade piece.

A fusion of indigenous and European ceramic traditions began in the sixteenth century, when the Spanish introduced the potter's wheel, a double-fired process allowing for a clean white background upon which to paint the new polychromatic tin glazes, and designs with Islamic, European, and Asian influences. In Europe, this pottery was known as *mayólica,* though it was renamed *talavera* in the New World in honor of the town where it originated, Talavera de la Reina, Spain. Today, only a handful of ceramic studios in Puebla follow the strict guidelines that allow them to produce "true" *talavera,* but towns such as Dolores Hidalgo produce a plethora of extremely popular *talavera*-style ceramics. Production of *mayólica,* however, spread to other parts of Mexico, most notably the colonial city of Guanajuato, where the Spanish tradition of twice-glazed pottery is carried on by two living masters: Gorky Gonzales and Javier de Jesús Hernandez (known by his studio name of Capelo). Son of a talented potter, and father to yet another, Gorky's enduring style remains true to old-school *mayólica*—the shapes classic, the colors muted, the designs simple. Renaissance man Capelo is an architect, sculptor, ceramicist, equestrian, and painter, and his mountaintop studio produces *mayólica* pieces that reveal his painterly ways, decorated with flowers and fruits, horses and birds, angels and mortals, all adroitly glazed on hand-thrown plates and pots.

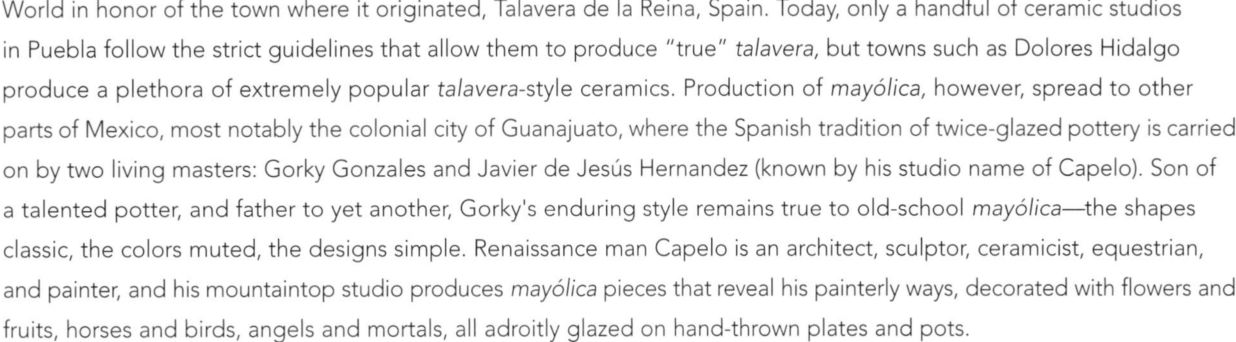

The rural Michoacán villages of Patamban and San José de Gracia are home to a prolific ceramic center where today's potters use the same firing methods as their pre-Hispanic forebears to create utilitarian and decorative pottery. Designs have evolved over time—an unexpected pineapple-shaped pot began to appear in the 1930s, for instance—but the ceramics produced in these villages today represent a legacy of purely Mexican art passed down through the ages.

In all four of the striking kitchens featured here, the owners' extensive pottery collections take center stage, expressing a beautiful and useful link to Mexico's rich ceramic heritage.

right, top. The road through San José de Gracia was paved a few years back, but when the owners made their first forays there it required a three-hour spine-jolting trip from the nearest town. The bowl holding the limes was purchased on one such early trip; the ram, like the paved road, is a more recent development.

right, bottom. The *piñas* (pineapples) atop the cabinets are from San José de Gracia, where many families produce these stylized pieces in simple workshops behind their homes. When they originated in the 1930s, the *piñas* were simple glazed jars decorated with rough daubs of clay. Over time the adornment has become more sophisticated, and the "leaves" are now often mold-made. On the counter is the work of Neftalí Ayungua from Patamban, where ceramicists also use deep-green glazes and often feature animal motifs.

page 118. In the elegant yet rustic kitchen of Casa de Hypatia in San Miguel de Allende, the owners' passion for Michoacán crafts is evident in their extensive collection of green-glazed ceramics and the masterfully carved woodwork that fill the room. The wooden column and brace on the left are originals from Tzintzuntzan, a carving village on the shores of Lake Pátzcuaro; a local master fashioned the chip-carved cabinets and beams and stained them the same deep rich brown to match. Classic cobalt-and-cream *talavera* tiles lavishly cover the counters and walls below a vaulted brick *bóveda* (domed) ceiling.

page 119. This stunning example of the exacting decorative work of San José de Gracia is by Hilario Alejos. Most *piñas* are glazed in green, some in gold, but select pieces like this punch bowl with hanging cups are finished in a distinctive deep blue.

above. Blue-and-white canisters from Dolores Hidalgo complement the lushly tiled counter and sink. Thirty years ago on a trip to Puebla, the interior designer–owner fell in love with this tile pattern and bought a few samples; years later she brought one to artist Penny Baker, in Dolores Hidalgo, who replicated and antiqued them, giving them a lustrous warm patina that belies their age.

left, top. A modern restaurant-quality stove is surrounded by timeless pieces of ceramic art. The large blue-and-white jar above the stove was the first piece in Hypatia's collection, purchased forty years ago in Dolores Hidalgo.

left. The blue-and-green theme continues into the formal dining room of Casa de Hypatia, where Peruvian religious images in gilt frames line stucco walls rag washed with spring green. The decorative wooden shutters on the windows and door were created by master artisan Juan David Guerra, inspired by those of a Franciscan monastery in Zacatecas.

above. Just off the tree-lined main square of Tlaxcala, behind a high stucco wall and through a diminutive wooden door, lies Casa Ramos, where the owner—Tlaxcaltecan through and through—has filled her kitchen with the tools of her trade; she is both chef and culinary anthropologist.

opposite, top left and right. Rustic pine shelves hold a plethora of dishware, old and new.

opposite, bottom. Nesting *casuelas* (cooking dishes) on the range are as attractive as they are useful.

opposite. The historic kitchen hearth at Casa Encantada in Pátzcuaro is decorated with rustic six-sided painted cement tiles. The arched alcove above holds a splendid collection of antique greenware from Patamban, some thought to be a hundred years old.

right, top. Modern ceramic figures by Marlene Johansing, entitled *Niña* and *Paz,* grace the kitchen of Casa Encantada. A hand-forged copper vase from Taller el Portón in Santa Clara de Cobre holds fiery-red gladiolas.

right, middle. These priceless pieces are considered *cerámica corriente,* meaning that they were made for everyday use. The style has become highly desirable in the international market, and lead-free glazes that will allow global shipments are now being developed.

right, bottom. In the village of Capula, almost everyone makes either pointillist pottery or *catrinas*—ceramic figures of elegantly dressed skeleton women with impossibly delicate fingers and features. Created by artist Guadalupe Posada in 1913, the *catrina* was originally meant as a satirical jab at the Mexican aristocracy, but she has since become an icon of Day of the Dead folk art.

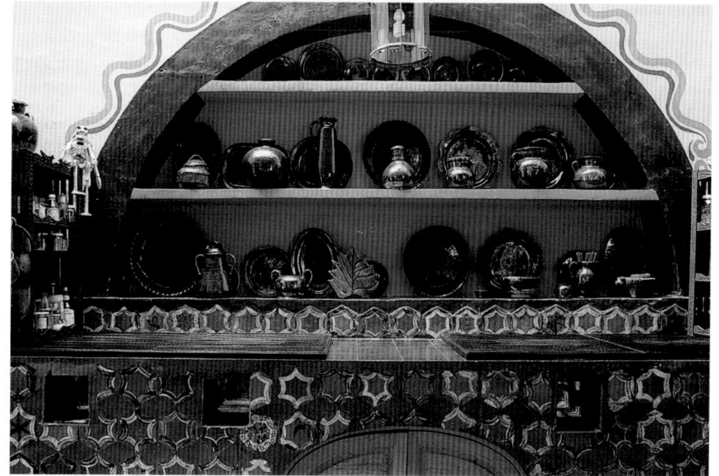

Casa Estrella

above. In the dining area, a stunning eight-foot tile mural by Capelo fills an alcove with a painterly image of the Sierra Madre Mountains, visible from the windows of Casa Estrella.

left. Perfectly framed by a recessed niche, pottery by Guanajuato master Gorky Gonzales is on display. Muted colors like these are characteristic of traditional *mayólica* and are fine examples of the work produced at Gorky's studio.

opposite. Custom-made tiles from Dolores Hidalgo spell out "Casa Estrella" over the range in this mountainside bed-and-breakfast in the hills overlooking Guanajuato. Glass shelves display the ceramic collection and allow the walls of decorative tiles to shine.

above. Natural light from numerous skylights draws the eye to a collection of earthenware pieces from Michoacán resting on a decorative brick shelf high above the kitchen. A wooden pig adds a humorous touch.

left. Life imitates art in this still life tableau. Classic *mayólica* pieces by Gorky Gonzales hold sumptuous fresh papaya, melon, and grapes, re-creating the images in the skillfully painted tiles by Capelo.

Boneless Chicken Breast with Orange-Chipotle Sauce

Pechuga de Pollo con Salsa de Naranja con Chipotle

INGREDIENTS

Serves 4

4 BONELESS CHICKEN BREAST HALVES (6 TO 8 OUNCES EACH)

3 CUPS ORANGE JUICE

1 TEASPOON SALT

2 MEDIUM SHALLOTS, MINCED

1 TABLESPOON BUTTER

1 CUP WHITE WINE

2 CUPS CHICKEN STOCK, PLUS MORE AS NEEDED (HOMEMADE IS BEST, BUT PREPARED LOW-SALT BROTH MAY BE SUBSTITUTED)

2 TABLESPOONS OLIVE OIL

3 TABLESPOONS CHOPPED FRESH CHIVES

2 CHIPOTLE CHILES *EN ADOBO*, SEEDS REMOVED AND CHILES FINELY CHOPPED

Brining chicken before cooking—bathing it in a sweet and salty solution—allows it to soak up flavor and moisture, guaranteeing a tastier finished product. Brining is usually done using water with copious amounts of sugar and salt added, but I prefer to use orange juice in place of water and sugar, and add just a bit of salt.

Chipotle chiles are smoked jalapeños, often found in supermarkets or Mexican markets canned *en adobo,* which means packed in a seasoned sauce. Their smoky flavor is beguiling, but their heat is mighty, so add them to the sauce just before serving, where they provide a hot spark in contrast to the sweet flavor of orange.

1 **To brine the chicken, put the breast halves in a sealable plastic bag** with 1 cup of the orange juice and the salt. Seal carefully, turn the bag to mix the brine thoroughly, and place the bag in a nonreactive bowl or baking pan. Chill for at least 2 hours or up to 6.

2 **To make the sauce, sauté the shallots in the butter** until they are softened but not browned. Add the wine and reduce to about ½ cup. Add the remaining 2 cups of orange juice and the chicken stock and bring to a boil over medium-high heat. Reduce the heat to low and simmer the sauce until it is reduced to about 1 cup and coats the back of a spoon. It will develop a shine at this point. The sauce may be made ahead to this point (cool, cover, and refrigerate for up to 2 hours) and reheated just before serving.

3 **Drain the chicken breasts and pat dry.** Heat the olive oil over medium-high heat in a sauté pan large enough to hold the chicken without crowding. When the pan is hot, add the chicken breasts and sear on both sides until they are nicely browned, then reduce the heat and cook, covered, until cooked through. The total cooking time will be 12 to 15 minutes, and an instant-read meat thermometer should read 165°F when inserted in the thickest part of a breast.

4 **To serve, reheat the sauce over medium heat** (add a splash of stock if it seems too thick). Slice the chicken breasts into ¾-inch-thick slices. (Each breast will yield about 5 slices.) Stir 2 tablespoons of the chives and the chipotle into the sauce. Place the chicken slices artfully on a serving platter or dinner plate and top with the sauce. Garnish with the remaining 1 tablespoon chives.

chapter 10

Lessons in History

Puebla's past lives on in the kitchens of the Amparo Museum, Casa de Alfeñique, Museum of the Revolution, and Santa Rosa Convent

RECIPE: STUFFED CHILES IN NUT SAUCE, CHILES EN NOGADA

Puebla's rich history began in 1531, just twelve years after Cortez's arrival in the New World. Planned by a Spanish urban designer, it was a city created for a purpose—to provide a Spanish-held stopover between the centrally located capital and the bustling ports of Acapulco and Veracruz. An abundance of prized commodities were arriving in New Spain—exotic foods, seeds and spices, fine Asian porcelain, Renaissance-style furniture—carried across the seas in galleons from Europe and the Far East.

A new art form arrived as well, when tile makers from Talavera de la Reina, Spain, introduced their tin-glazed ceramics to proficient local potters. Puebla's famous *talavera* pottery was born, providing New Spain with earthenware for its tables and the city of Puebla with enough multicolored tiles to cover her baroque churches, cathedrals, government buildings, and homes inside and out, earning it the moniker "City of Tiles."

Aside from Puebla's great significance in Mexican history—it was the site of the legendary Battle of Puebla on May 5, 1862, and home to some of the first casualties of the Mexican Revolution—it is honored as a culinary center as well, for two of Mexico's most revered dishes—*mole poblano* and *chiles en nogada*—were born here. Their flavors capture the unique style of Puebla—deep indigenous roots flavored with exotic and sophisticated Moorish, European, and Asian influences. The historic *poblano* kitchens found in Puebla's museums, four of which are featured here, are lasting reminders of Puebla's celebrated past and contributions to the present.

above. The Amparo Museum houses a classic *poblano* kitchen: *talavera* tiles on the floor, a deeply inset door with a decorative arch, and a collection of earthenware plates and pots.

left. Hexagonal terra-cotta tiles mix with *talavera* tiles to brighten the kitchen floor. Large cooking vessels like these, as well as wood for the fire, were often stored under the hearth at floor level.

opposite. Four traditional implements used in making tortillas: a flat stone *metate* with a *mano* (rolling pin) to grind *nixtamal* (dried corn soaked in water and slaked lime), wooden tortilla presses for making uniform tortillas with less work than those *hecho a mano* (made by hand), a round wooden *marcador* (a carved stamp used to press designs into fresh tortillas for special occasions), and a flat wooden bowl *(palangana)* to hold fresh water.

page 130. The Amparo Museum, located in the historic central district of Puebla, houses a stunning collection of art from pre-Hispanic to contemporary. The *virreinal* (colonial) collection, exhibited in the second-floor living quarters of the restored mansion, includes sacred and secular work, furniture, and the colonial kitchen shown here.

page 131. *Casuelas* (cooking dishes) hang from the tile and stucco kitchen walls.

above. When the Spanish introduced wheat — and a taste for bread — to the New World, beehive ovens like this one appeared.

left. The facade of the Casa de Alfeñique, built in 1790, is ornately decorated with baroque plaster decorations that resemble fluffy spun sugar (*alfeñique* comes from the Arabic word for sweets or candy). In the third-floor kitchen, the raised hearth and hood above it are painted a traditional terra-cotta red. Kitchens of this era were often located on upper floors so that the noise and smells involved in making meals wouldn't disturb the nobles housed below.

opposite, top. Tiles adorn the stucco kitchen walls, along with ceramic oh-so-French boots.

opposite, bottom. Under a wooden shelf filled with plates, a table is lavishly covered in *talavera* tiles.

left. Surrounded by gleaming tiles in a multitude of colors, designs, and patterns, San Pasqual Bailón blesses the cooks and their kitchen.

page 136. Mexico is home to many museums dedicated to the Mexican Revolution, but only Puebla's is the site of the revolution's first armed conflict, the building's facade still scarred with holes from bullets fired in 1910. Converted into a museum in 1960 to commemorate the heroic deeds of the Serdán family, the second-story kitchen was restored and is now a showcase of *talavera* tiles and *poblano* pottery.

page 137. Earthenware pitchers and jugs lining a tiled shelf over the large six-burner stove are glazed in brown and black, a classic Puebla pottery style.

above. Through the years, some tiles have broken and been replaced, but these original tiles are a testament to their durability, still vibrantly gleaming after more than three hundred years.

left. The eight-pointed star, repeated throughout the Santa Rosa kitchen, is an ancient Islamic design, often seen in Spanish tiles, that was passed on to Mexico.

opposite. Religious orders were esteemed in New Spain, their convents well financed by the new nobility. With access to all manner of ingredients owing to the trade passing through Puebla, friars and nuns well versed in the culinary arts were able to woo their benefactors with lavish meals, imported wines, and decadent desserts. In Puebla, nuns were known for the wide array of sweets they concocted as well as rich sauces made with chiles. Legend has it that in the barrel-vaulted kitchen of the Convent of Santa Rosa pictured here, a nun and her indigenous cooks used the pre-Hispanic tradition of grinding together chiles, nuts, seeds, and vegetables, then added exotic spices from the Orient and—in a moment of perhaps divine inspiration—chocolate, creating the dish for which Puebla is most famous: *mole poblano.* Legend also says that in gratitude for this complex and sophisticated dish, the bishop ordered the convent kitchen to be tiled floor to ceiling in the colorful *talavera* tiles for which Puebla was famous.

above. Historically, hearths were at floor level, a simple affair of three rocks on which to rest a pot over a fire burning in the hollow. The raised stove, here clad in a glorious mix of tiles, was a later development in kitchens that allowed for a greater degree of control over the fire as well as more ease in moving the pots and pans.

left. Tiled counters near the hearth provide space for large cooking pots to cool.

opposite, left. A tiled *nicho* built into the wall of the convent kitchen holds ingredients and utensils. Water was stored in large earthenware jars, known as *tinajas,* like the decorative one seen here on the right.

opposite, right. A wooden holder filled with well-worn spoons in the convent kitchen.

Stuffed Chiles in Nut Sauce

Chiles en Nogada

This traditional dish from Puebla is often served on September 16, Mexico's Independence Day. The green of the roasted chiles, the white of the creamy nut sauce, and the red of the glistening pomegranate seeds represent the colors of the Mexican flag.

The meat filling, called *picadillo,* calls for a candied cactus called *biznaga,* which is readily available in Mexico but unlikely to be found in the States. Unless you brought some home from your last visit to Mexico, you'll need to substitute candied pineapple. *Piloncillo,* the unrefined Mexican sugar that is sold in cone shapes, may be replaced with dark brown sugar.

This dish is usually served at room temperature, but if you prefer, as I do, you may heat the stuffed chiles and gently warm the sauce before serving.

INGREDIENTS

Serves 12

12 POBLANO CHILES

1 MEDIUM WHITE OR YELLOW ONION, CHOPPED

4 CLOVES GARLIC, FINELY CHOPPED

1 TABLESPOON PURE OLIVE OIL

2 POUNDS GROUND PORK (YOU MAY SUBSTITUTE TURKEY FOR SOME OR ALL OF THE PORK)

1 ALMOST RIPE PLANTAIN, PEELED AND CHOPPED

1 APPLE, PEELED AND CHOPPED

1 PEACH, PEELED AND CHOPPED

1 PEAR, PEELED AND CHOPPED

ONE 28-OUNCE CAN CHOPPED TOMATOES

¼ CUP RAISINS

2 TABLESPOONS *BIZNAGA* (OR SUBSTITUTE CANDIED PINEAPPLE)

1 CINNAMON STICK, BROKEN INTO PIECES

½ TEASPOON GROUND CLOVES

3 TABLESPOONS *PILONCILLO* (OR SUBSTITUTE DARK BROWN SUGAR)

3 TABLESPOONS VINEGAR OR LIME JUICE

SALT AND FRESHLY GROUND BLACK PEPPER TO TASTE

4 CUPS NUT SAUCE, *recipe follows*

SEEDS OF 1 POMEGRANATE

12 SPRIGS ITALIAN PARSLEY FOR GARNISH

1 **Place the chiles over an open flame** (the burner on a gas stove works well for this, or use your barbeque grill), and use tongs to turn them frequently until the skins are blistered and slightly charred. Place the chiles in a paper bag and wrap the bag with a clean kitchen towel for 5 minutes. Carefully remove the skins and seeds, leaving the stems intact. To get the seeds out, cut a vertical slit in the side of a chile and remove the seeds and the veins, being careful to leave the chiles whole so that you can stuff them. (At this point, if the chiles seem too spicy for your taste, you can soak them in water to cover with some salt and vinegar. Mexican cooks say that this can reduce the heat of a chile.) These can be prepared a day ahead of serving and kept, well wrapped, in the refrigerator.

2 **Sauté the onion and garlic** in the oil over medium heat in a large sauté pan until softened. Add the ground pork, all the chopped fruits, and the tomatoes, and cook, stirring often, until the pork is cooked through. Add the raisins, *biznaga*, cinnamon, cloves, *piloncillo*, vinegar, and salt and pepper, stir well to combine, and cook for about 15 minutes to meld the flavors. Check and adjust the seasonings. This is best made a day ahead of serving (transfer to a bowl, cover, and refrigerate).

3 **The day of serving, carefully stuff each chile with the meat filling (*picadillo*).** Place the chiles in a baking dish (microwavable, if you're going to serve them hot) and chill until 1 hour before serving time.

4 To serve cool, bring the chiles and nut sauce to room temperature. **To serve hot,** bring the chiles to room temperature, cover the baking dish with a paper towel, and microwave the chiles until they are heated through. The time required will depend on your microwave, but start with 10 minutes on high, turning the dish once midway. Heat the nut sauce slowly while the chiles are reheating.

Hot or cold, to serve, place the chiles on a serving platter with the stems all facing the same direction, or on individual dinner plates. Stir the nut sauce and pour it in a thick band over the center of the chiles. Sprinkle the pomegranate seeds on the sauce (you may not need them all) and garnish with the parsley.

Nut Sauce

Put the milk and nuts in a glass container and warm them in the microwave. The time will vary depending on your microwave, but about 10 minutes on medium-high is a good start. Soak the nuts in the warmed milk for 30 minutes to soften them. Put the nuts, milk, cream cheese, *queso fresco,* sherry, cinnamon, and salt and white pepper in a blender and blend until velvety smooth. Pour the sauce through a strainer to remove any tough skins. This sauce thickens as it sits, so don't be concerned if it seems thin.

Nut Sauce

Makes 4 cups

2 CUPS WHOLE MILK

2 CUPS NUTS (A MIXTURE OF PECANS, ALMONDS, AND WALNUTS IS BEST)

3 OUNCES CREAM CHEESE

8 OUNCES *QUESO FRESCO* (AVAILABLE IN MEXICAN MARKETS AND MANY LARGE GROCERY STORES; SEE PAGE 89)

2 TABLESPOONS DRY SHERRY

¼ TEASPOON GROUND CINNAMON, OR MORE TO TASTE

SALT AND WHITE PEPPER TO TASTE

right. In a charming hand-painted tile mosaic of kitchen saint San Pasqual Bailón, "I make the stew and you add the seasoning" implies that although the cook may prepare the stew, San Pasqual is the one who makes it delicious.

chapter II

Islands in Time

Unique designs in the kitchens of Casa Gaudí, Casa Oaxaca, and Casa de los Milagros

RECIPE: CHOCOLATE CHILE TRUFFLES, *TRUFAS DE CHOCOLATE CON CHILE*

Contemporary Mexican kitchens represent a union of innovative new ideas and time-honored traditions: ultramodern appliances share space with pre-Hispanic tools, slick stainless steel coexists with hand-hewn wood, and polished concrete countertops in a range of colors complement the age-old glazes of *talavera* tiles.

Freestanding cooking surfaces, often horseshoe shaped, were not uncommon in colonial Mexico, and these three up-to-date counterparts prove their lasting worth. Kitchen islands offer a convenient location for a sink or cooktop, desirable extra storage space, and often a spot for casual dining. Task-specific countertops—butcher block for chopping, granite or marble for pastry making—allow the owners to adapt the island to their requirements.

Arriving at Casa Gaudí, one wonders if the taxi leaving colonial San Miguel de Allende took a detour to Barcelona. This exuberant homage to Spain's most famous contemporary architect screams "fun!" in every wild and wacky detail. In the thoroughly modern kitchen, stainless steel, glass, tile, and stone collaborate to create a bright and beautiful workspace.

Behind a simple door on a bustling street in the heart of Oaxaca lies a peaceful oasis: Casa Oaxaca. The stylish seven-room inn and courtyard restaurant offer the visitor sophisticated decor and innovative dining within its seventeenth-century walls. In the elegantly designed kitchen, chef Alejandro Ruíz creates contemporary Mexican dishes using ingredients both new and old, and diners flock to partake of his *nueva cocina Mexicana.*

Stringent local laws regarding the destruction of historical buildings in Oaxaca kept the owner of Casa de los Milagros waiting twenty years to build her dream house on the site of her husband's family home. Only after the old structure collapsed completely in an earthquake was she able to build her house of miracles. Completed in 2002, Casa de los Milagros now operates as an intimate bed-and-breakfast, sister inn to Las Bugambilias, and cooking classes for the guests are often held in the spacious kitchen.

opposite, left. An asymmetrical see-through glass table offers casual seating in front of Casa Gaudí's marble-topped island. Above the cooktop, the stylish hood of glass and steel wraps practical purpose in bold design. On the back wall, the tall stainless-steel column is actually a pullout storage pantry for dry goods.

opposite, top right. Rope lights are set into the archway framing the dining nook, where a gas-fired pizza-bread oven was installed.

opposite, bottom right. Shards of tiles in shades of blue form a mosaic around the pizza oven set into the outside wall. Just a flip of a switch fires up the gas-fired oven.

right, top. A porthole window of textured stained glass brightens the far wall in stripes of yellow and red. The black marble counter-tops throughout the kitchen were chosen for their chic style, but just as important are their durability and easy cleanup. The central island includes a five-burner stovetop, plenty of workspace, and hidden storage below.

right, bottom. Stainless-steel panels cover the kitchen walls in industrial simplicity; the multi-colored espresso cups, with their flower-petal saucers, provide a soft and whimsical balance.

page 146. A thoroughly Moorish arch, the only nod to history in sight, frames azure walls and gleaming stainless steel in the kitchen of Casa Gaudí. Ultramodern appliances, glass-fronted cabinets, and stainless-steel wall panels were imported from Spain and Germany to complete the owners' dream of bringing cutting-edge design to colonial Mexico.

page 147. Modern blue cooking utensils hang from a stainless-steel rod conveniently placed on the island.

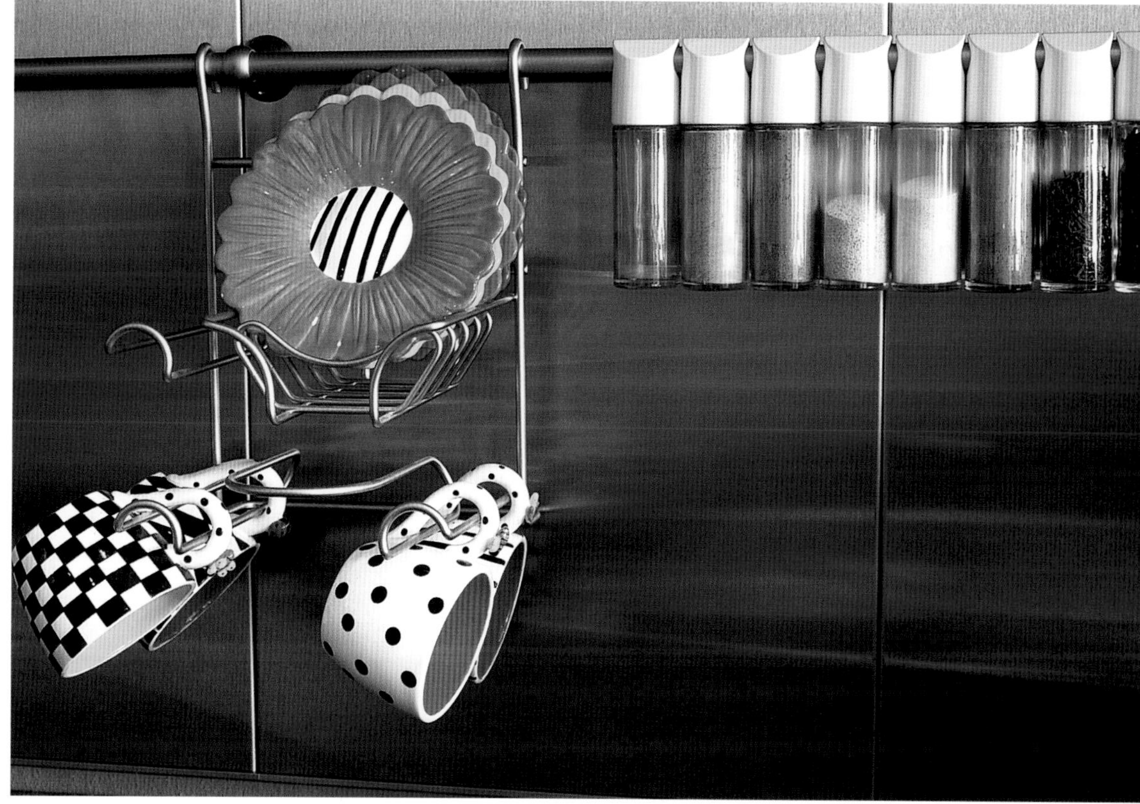

above. Though both these tiles are made from the same clay, the methods for finishing them are different: the *talavera* tiles on the wall were given a white undercoat to hide the color of the clay and to provide a clean painting surface, while the six-sided unglazed floor tiles were left in their natural earthen state.

left. A glass-doored cupboard holds earthenware dishes used by the restaurant.

opposite, top. A moment of calm is rare in the usually bustling kitchen, where Alejandro Ruiz performs his culinary magic for diners at Casa Oaxaca's alfresco restaurant. Two levels of the island double its usefulness by providing a lower prep area and an upper display level.

opposite, bottom. Traditional Oaxacan clay dishes like these are used to serve Casa Oaxaca's new classics.

pages 150–151. The sleek and stylish kitchen of Casa Oaxaca offers up contemporary Oaxacan cuisine, an imaginative spin on time-honored culinary traditions. The gracefully curved island is unusual to find in a restaurant kitchen, where its warm wood top softens the austerity of the white tiled walls.

opposite. Warm yellow marble forms the countertop of the large U-shaped island at Casa de los Milagros where guests gather for cooking demonstrations. A four-burner cooktop and prep sink set into the island allow students to observe each step of the preparation. The stylish wooden bench (as well as the dining table and chairs) were designed and executed by the Italian-Oaxacan furniture manufacturer Mobili Piave.

left, top. Discovered in an antique shop in Puebla, this pot rack was originally used in a *carnicería* (butcher shop) to hang freshly made chorizo for aging.

left, bottom. A magnetic rack holds a selection of sharp knives against a gleaming deep-blue tile backsplash.

above. A colorfully set table welcomes guests to the sunlit kitchen of Casa de los Milagros. Wooden doors and matching *alacenas* (kitchen cupboards) on both side walls were crafted by local artisans.

Chocolate Chile Truffles

Trufas de Chocolate con Chile

INGREDIENTS

Makes about 48 truffles

1 CUP HEAVY CREAM

3 TABLESPOONS UNSALTED BUTTER, CUT INTO PIECES

3 TO 4 TEASPOONS ANCHO CHILE POWDER

1 POUND FINE-QUALITY BITTERSWEET CHOCOLATE, CHOPPED

1 CUP UNSWEETENED DUTCH-PROCESS COCOA POWDER

Chocolate and chile have been eaten in Mexico since pre-Hispanic times. Montezuma was said to have imbibed copious amounts of a bitter spicy beverage each day. This wonderful recipe by Lisa Gahafer combines those two flavors again, this time in chocolate truffles with the unexpected flavor of ancho chile. At first bite the chocolate reigns, but slowly the heat from the chiles begins to open on your palate, and the combination of hot, sweet, and chocolate is divine.

These are best made at least a day ahead to give the flavors time to ripen. You can double or triple the recipe and store the truffles, coated in cocoa, in the freezer for up to one month.

1 Bring the cream and butter to a simmer over medium heat in a small heavy saucepan and stir in the ancho chile powder. Remove from heat and let steep for several minutes.

2 Place the chopped chocolate in a microwavable bowl, preferably glass. Pour the warm cream mixture over the chocolate and heat in the microwave at 50 percent power for 2 minutes. Stir the chocolate and cream together. If the chocolate is not quite melted, microwave again at 50 percent power in 30-second increments until it is melted. Stir to combine completely. Chill the chocolate mixture, covered, until firm, for about 2 hours.

3 Let the chocolate mixture sit at room temperature for 1 hour before you form the truffles. Spoon level teaspoons of the chocolate onto a baking sheet. Put cocoa into a bowl, dust your palms lightly with the cocoa, and roll each piece of chocolate into a ball. Drop the balls into the bowl of cocoa and turn them gently to coat evenly. Reserve the remaining cocoa powder for serving.

Make at least a day in advance and store in an airtight container, separating the layers with wax paper. Before serving, roll the truffles again in the reserved cocoa powder to coat. For the best flavor, serve at room temperature.

chapter 12

Class Act

Cooking school kitchens at Seasons of My Heart, Patsy's Place, and Los Dos

RECIPE: BAKED CUSTARD WITH CARAMEL SAUCE, FLAN CLÁSICO

Susana Trilling's culinary interest began early in her Mexican-born grandmother's kitchen in Texas, a room she thought as a child was the "center of the universe." After years spent working as a chef in the United States, Susana relocated to Rancho Aurora, a hillside farm in the glorious fertile valley of Oaxaca. There she is raising her family and managing her popular cooking school, Seasons of My Heart. In her spacious and well-designed classroom kitchen—her "temple of food," as her friends call it—she shares her passion and knowledge of traditional Oaxacan cooking with all who enter.

Patsy Dubois arrived in San Miguel de Allende in the 1970s to study art at the Instituto Allende, an art and language school founded by a group of local Mexicans and expatriate North Americans. Her path led to Mexico City, where she taught English to the family of a Mexican president—and learned the ways of *la cocina Mexicana*—but eventually she found her way back to a ranch in the countryside outside San Miguel. While she appreciated the charms of the local colonial architecture, she always dreamed of having a contemporary kitchen in which to teach her popular "country cooking" classes, and in 2004 Patsy's Place became a reality.

Chef David Sterling of Los Dos Cooking School in the capital city of Mérida, Yucatán, was developing a line of exotic Mexican-influenced condiments in New York City when the urge struck to move to warmer climes. He and his partner, Keith, packed up their possessions and took flight to Mérida, a town whose languorous pace, Old World style, and complex cuisine intrigued them both. Yucatecan cuisine blends the flavors of Spain, France, and the Caribbean with indigenous Mayan ingredients and preparation methods, and David and Keith designed their home with this synthesis in mind. In classes held in his elegant kitchen, a tropical fan twirling above and French floor tiles below, David introduces food-loving visitors to the complex flavors of Yucatán.

above. These paper-star lanterns are made in India, but their color and style are right at home in Mexico. Hanging from the skylight, they fill the domed *bóveda* ceiling with their bright colors.

left. Beyond a floral painted arch, the bright and spacious kitchen at Seasons of My Heart includes several separate task areas, allowing many people at a time to work both efficiently and independently.

page 158. An island of stone and tile serves as Susana's stage when she introduces the day's recipes. The various earthenware vessels are the everyday pots and pans of rural Mexico, used on the stove or over an open fire to cook everything from hot chocolate to rice and beans.

page 159. A rustic triple-tiered basket of woven vines holds fruits and vegetables.

above. A close-up of the island front displays the contrast of natural stone and manmade tile. Modern tile motifs such as the *sol* (sun) and the *girasol* (sunflower, which delightfully translates to "turn to the sun") are the products of *talavera*-style tile factories in Dolores Hidalgo.

left. Contrasting the modern with the traditional, a professional-quality range sits under a brilliant blue stucco hood adorned with floral painting and a tile mosaic of the Virgin of Guadalupe.

opposite, top. Susana's husband, Eric, grows organic vegetables such as these in the rich loam of the Oaxaca Valley. The basket on the right holds husked tomatillos, a member of the gooseberry family (hence the papery husk) indigenous to Mexico. They are known by numerous names in different regions of Mexico: *tomate verde* in the central highlands, *tomate de hoja* in the Sierra Gorda, and *miltomate* in Oaxaca, among others.

opposite, bottom. Lava rock mortars, *molcajetes,* are a staple of every Mexican kitchen, used with a pestle to grind ingredients for salsas. Their makers take part in carving contests, and these prizewinners are clearly from the victorious Oaxaqueño team.

OAXAC

above. The scale of the kitchen is grand, matching the sweeping landscape of the high desert just beyond the walls. With plenty of room for storage on the well-organized shelves, the kitchen remains uncluttered. Students gather around large poured-concrete worktables for hands-on preparation of their meal.

opposite. The spacious light-filled kitchen of Patsy's Place is blushed with sunlight from the Barragánesque skylights. At lunchtime, students will enjoy the fruits of their labor seated at the dining table topped with bright Mexican oilcloth and fresh flowers from the garden.

left, top. Many chefs think of their stoves as altars, and Patsy's — in its own tiled-covered alcove, illumined by skylights above—is no exception. Glazed Saltillo tiles cover the floor; sage-green tiles on the walls were purchased at Artesana, a home decor store in San Miguel de Allende.

left, bottom. Before classes begin, students choose their favorite apron from this colorful selection collected in Patsy's travels.

opposite. The kitchen at Los Dos is magnificent in scale, color, and design. Its most innovative feature is the circular central island, with its bi-level countertop. Opulently covered with tile from the *talavera* factories of Puebla, it is an inspired piece of kitchen architecture, offering counter space on the upper level and seating on the lower.

left. A circular iron rack over the island keeps the counter clear and pots and pans nearby. Note the dishwasher built into the island on the right.

below. The distinctive striped pattern of the tiles above the stove represents the House of Bourbon that long ruled Spain. David brought the decorative tile coat of arms, depicting Spanish heraldry, to Mérida from Madrid.

opposite, top left. Andalusian influences from southern Spain are evident in the Moorish designs of the wooden cabinet details.

opposite, top right. Tiles covering the walls are from Puebla, their intricate geometric designs made even more dramatic by their creative placement. The painted cement floor tiles were rescued from the home's original kitchen. They arrived in Mérida from France after serving as ballast on a cargo ship crossing the seas. Today, Materiales Traqui, in nearby Ucu, Yucatán, produces stunning cement tiles such as these in custom colors and designs.

opposite, bottom right. The basic designs of these three-legged stone grinding instruments—the bowl-shaped *molcajetes* and a rectangular *metate*—have not changed since pre-Hispanic times. Before use, they are cured by grinding several times with raw rice or dried corn to smooth the surface. As evidenced by the ancient *metate* pictured here, once cured, they will last a lifetime.

left. The bounty of Mexico's farmlands and orchards is ready to be transformed into a Yucatecan specialty in the kitchen of Los Dos.

above. In the formal dining room just off the kitchen, a local painter took three weeks, working ten hours a day, to complete this charming mural depicting daily life in Mérida, right down to the Mayan pyramids in the countryside.

Baked Custard with Caramel Sauce

Flan Clásico

INGREDIENTS

Serves 8

I CUP SUGAR

I CUP EVAPORATED OR FRESH MILK

I CUP HEAVY CREAM

I CUP SWEETENED CONDENSED MILK

I VANILLA BEAN (OPTIONAL)

2 EGGS, PLUS 3 EGG YOLKS

2 TEASPOONS PURE MEXICAN VANILLA EXTRACT

Brought to Mexico by the Spanish, who found their inspiration in France's crème caramel, flan has been so completely integrated into *la cocina Mexicana* that it is now commonly considered a purely Mexican dish.

You will need to work quickly when spreading the caramel syrup in the mold, as it hardens rapidly. As the custard bakes, the caramel softens, forming a delicious amber sauce that is released when the flan is unmolded.

Lisa Gahafer, a talented American chef who spends her summers catering in the Napa Valley and her winters in San Miguel de Allende teaching cooking classes, shared this wonderful recipe with me.

1 **Preheat the oven to 325°F.**

2 **Add the sugar to a small dry skillet or heavy saucepan** and cook over medium heat to melt. Cook until you have a clear, deep amber liquid, 8 to 10 minutes. Remove from the heat and, working quickly, pour into a shallow mold or 8 individual ramekins, tilting to distribute the caramel evenly on the bottom and the sides of the mold.

3 **Combine the milk, cream, and condensed milk in a saucepan** over medium heat. Split the vanilla bean (if using) lengthwise and use the tip of a paring knife to scrape the seeds into the milk mixture. Add the bean and bring the mixture just to a boil. Remove from the heat and let cool.

4 **In a small bowl, whisk together the eggs and egg yolks until well blended.** Slowly pour the eggs into the cooled milk mixture, whisking constantly. Stir in the vanilla extract.

5 **Pour the egg and milk mixture through a strainer** into the caramel-coated mold or divide equally among ramekins. Place the mold or ramekins inside a larger baking pan and put in the preheated oven. Add boiling water to the outer baking pan, halfway up the sides of the flan mold. Bake the flan in the water bath for 45 minutes to 1 hour (35 to 40 minutes for individual ramekins), or until it no longer trembles in the center when moved. Remove from the oven and let cool in the water bath. Remove from the bath, cover the mold or ramekins with plastic wrap, and chill.

6 **To serve, run a knife along the inside edge of the mold,** cover with a platter, invert the mold onto the platter, and cut into wedges; invert ramekins onto individual plates.

Casa de Alfeñique
Esq. 4 Oriente y 6 Norte, Col. Centro
Puebla, Puebla 72000
52+222-232-0458 T

Casa de las Bugambilias
Reforma #402, Col. Centro
Oaxaca, Oaxaca 68000
52+951-516-1165 T and F
in U.S. 321-249-9422
bugambilias@lasbugambilias.com
www.lasbugambilias.com

Casa Encantada
Dr. Coss #15, Col. Centro
Pátzcuaro, Michoacán 61600
52+434-342-3492 T
in U.S. 619-819-8398
victoria@lacasaencantada.com
www.lacasaencantada.com

Casa de Espíritus Alegres
Ex-Hacienda la Trinidad #1, Col. Marfil
Guanajuato, Guanajuato 36250
52+473-733-1013 T and F
info@casaspirit.com
www.casaspirit.com

Casa Estrella de la Valenciana
Callejón Jalisco #10, Mineral de Valenciana
Guanajuato, Guanajuato 36240
52+473-732-1784
in U.S. 886-983-8844
info@mexicaninns.com
www.mexicaninns.com

Casa Felipe Flores
Dr. Jose Felipe Flores #36, Col. Centro
San Cristóbal de las Casas, Chiapas 29230
52+967-678-3996 T and F
nodomaya@felipeflores.com
www.felipeflores.com

Casa Luna Pila Seca
Pila Seca #11, Col. Centro
Casa Luna Quebrada
Quebrada #117, Col. Centro
San Miguel de Allende, Guanajuato 37700
52+415-152-1117 T and F
in U.S. 210-200-8758
casaluna@unisono.net.mx
www.casaluna.com

Casa de los Milagros
Matamoros #500-C, Col. Centro
Oaxaca, Oaxaca 68000
52+951-501-2262 T, 52+951-515-7745 F
casadelosmilagros@hotmail.com
www.mexonline.com/milagros.htm

Casa Oaxaca
García Vigil #407, Col. Centro
Oaxaca, Oaxaca 68000
52+951-514-4173 T, 52+951-516-4412 F
casaoaxaca@prodigy.net.mx
www.casa-oaxaca.com

Casa de la Real Aduana
Ponce de León #16, Col. Centro
Pátzcuaro, Michoacán 61600
52+434-342-0265 T and F
real_aduana@lafoliamx.com
www.lafoliamx.com

Casa de los Sabores
Libres #205, Col. Centro
Oaxaca, Oaxaca 68000
52+951-516-5704 T and F
bugambilias2@yahoo.com
www.mexonline.com/sabores.htm

Casa Santana
Calle 64 #410, x47 y49, Col. Centro
Mérida, Yucatán 97300
52+999-928-7567 T
casasantana410@hotmail.com
www.casasantana.com

Ex-Convento de Santa Rosa
3 Norte x 14 Poniente, Col. Centro
Puebla, Puebla 72000
52+222-232-9240 T

A Cook's Tour of Mexico
4061 Mandeville Canyon Road
Los Angeles, CA 90049
310-440-8877 T, 310-471-0163 F
nancy@nancyzaslavsky.com
www.nancyzaslavsky.com

Culinary Adventures
6023 Reid Dr. NW
Gig Harbor, WA 98335
253-851-7676 T, 253-851-9532 F
marilyntausend@comcast.net
www.marilyntausend.com

Fundación Cultural Rodolfo Morales
Av. Morelos #108
Ocotlán de Morelos, Oaxaca 71151
52+951-571-0198 T and F
fundacionmorales@hotmail.com

Gabriela Gudiño Gual, tour guide
Calzada México #81, Barrio de Fatima
San Cristóbal de las Casas, Chiapas 29264
52+967-678-4223 T and F
gggual@hotmail.com

Hacienda Chichén Resort
Chichén Itzá, Yucatán 97751
52+999-924-4222 T, 52+999-924-5011 F
in U.S. and Canada 877-631-4005
info@haciendachichen.com
www.haciendachichen.com

Hacienda San Gabriel de las Palmas
KM 41.8 Carr. Cuernavaca-Chilpancingo
Amacuzac, Morelos
52+751-348-0636 T, 52+751-348-0113 F
reservaciones@hacienda-sangabriel.com.mx
www.hacienda-sangabriel.com.mx

Hotel Casa Vieja México
Eugenio Sue #45, Col. Polanco
Mexico, D.F. 11560
52+55-5282-0067 T, 55-5281-3780 F
sales@casavieja.com
www.casavieja.com

Hotel Casavieja
Maria Adelina Flores #27, Col. Centro
San Cristóbal de las Casas, Chiapas 29230
52+967-678-6868 T and F
hcvieja@casavieja.com.mx
www.casavieja.com.mx

Hotel Casa del Balam
Calle 60 #488, Col. Centro
Mérida, Yucatán 97000
52+999-924-2150 T, 52+999-924-5011 F
in U.S. 800-624-8451
casadelbalam@prodigy.com.mx
www.casadelbalam.com

Las Mañanitas
Ricardo Linares #107, Col. Centro
Cuernavaca, Morelos 62000
52+777-314-1466 T, 52+777-318-3672 F
lasmananitas@lasmananitas.com.mx
www.lasmananitas.com.mx

La Mancha Bed and Breakfast
Plaza Ejército Libertador #8, Col. Parres
Cuernavaca, Morelos 62564
52+777-320-6621 T
in U.S. 619-840-5154
carolhop1@aol.com
www.lamanchasur.com

Los Dos Cooking School and Guest House
Calle 68 #517 x65 y67, Col. Centro
Mérida, Yucatán 97000
52+999-928-1116 T, 52+999-928-1115 F
in U.S. 212-400-1642
chefsterling@los-dos.com
www.los-dos.com

Mesón Sacristía de Capuchinas
9 Oriente #16 Col. Centro
Puebla, Puebla 72000
52+222-232-8088 T, 52+222-246-6084 F
toll-free in Mexico 800-712-4028
sacristía@mesones-sacristia.com
www.mesones-sacristia.com

Mesón Sacristía de la Compañía
Calle 6 Sur #304, Col. Centro
Puebla, Puebla 72000
52+222-242-3554 T, 52+222-232-4513 F
toll-free in Mexico 800-712-4028
sacristía@mesones-sacristia.com
www.mesones-sacristia.com

Mexican Home Cooking
Apdo. 64
Tlaxcala, Tlaxcala, 90000
52+246-468-0978 T and F
MexicanHomeCooking@yahoo.com
www.mexicanhomecooking.com

Museo Amparo
2 Sur #708, Col. Centro
Puebla, Puebla 72000
52+222-229-3850 T, 52+222-246-6333 F
amparo@museoamparo.com
www.museoamparo.com

Museo de Artes e Industrias Populares
Vasco de Quiroga x Arciga, Col. Centro
Pátzcuaro, Michoacán 61600
52+434-342-1029 T

Museo Robert Brady
Calle Netzahualcoyotl #4, Col. Centro
Cuernavaca, Morelos 62000
52+777-318-8554 T, 52+777-314-3529 F
museobrady@prodigy.net.mx
www.geocities.com/bradymuseum

Museo Dolores Olmedo Patiño
Av. Mexico #5843, Col. La Noria
Xochimilco, México, D.F. 16030
52+55-5555-0891 T, 52+55-5555-1642 F
museodoloresolmedo@hotmail.com

Museo de Frida Kahlo, Casa Azul
Londres #247 Col. del Carmen
Coyoacán, México, D.F. 04100
52+55-5554-5999 T, 52+55-5658-5778 F

Museo de la Revolución Mexicana
6 Oriente #206, Col. Centro
Puebla, Puebla 72000
52+222-242-1076 T

El Naranjo Restaurant and Cooking School
Valerio Trujano #203, Col. Centro
Oaxaca, Oaxaca 68000
52+951-514-1878 T
iliana@elnaranjo.com.mx
www.elnaranjo.com.mx

Patsy's Place
Apdo. #11
San Miguel de Allende, Guanajuato 37700
52+415-153-5303 or 52+415-185-2151 T
mexcooking@prodigy.net.mx
www.patsydubois.com

El Refugio en Pátzcuaro
Benigno Serrato #11, Col. Centro
Pátzcuaro, Michoacán 61600
52+434-342-5237 T and F
reservations@elrefugioenpatzcuaro.com.mx
www.elrefugioenpatzcuaro.com.mx

Carlos Rivero, tour guide
Priv. Díaz Ordaz #4305, Interior 1
Puebla, Puebla 72550
52+222-304-2855 T, 52+222-285-6868 F
carlos@riveros.com.mx
www.riveros.com.mx

Seasons of My Heart
Apdo. #42, Admon. 3
Oaxaca, Oaxaca 68101
52+951-508-0044 T and F
seasons@spersaoaxaca.com.mx
www.seasonsofmyheart.com

Susurro Bed and Breakfast
Recreo #78, Col. Centro
San Miguel de Allende, Guanajuato 37700
52+415-152-1065 T
in U.S. 323-449-6533
rwaters@earthlink.net
www.susurro.com.mx

La Villa del Ensueño
Florida #305, Col. San Pedro
Tlaquepaque, Jalisco 45500
52+333-635-8792 T, 52+333-659-6152 F
in U.S. 800-220-8689
reservaciones@villadelensueno.com
www.villadelensueno.com

Villa Montaña Hotel and Spa
Patzimba # 201 Col. Vista Bella
Morelia, Michoacán 58090
52+434-314-0231 T, 52+434-325-1423 F
in U.S. 800-223-6510
in Canada 800-448-8355
res@villamontana.com.mx
www.villamontana.com.mx

Azulejos Talavera Vásquez, tile and ceramics
Puebla #56 and #58, Col. Centro
Dolores Hidalgo, Guanajuato 37800
52+418-182-0630 T and F
jvasquez47324@hotmail.com

Marcia Bland Brown, interior design
Box 277 Allende 5
San Miguel de Allende, Guanajuato 37899
52+415-153-3176 T
in U.S. 210-785-9554 T
mbb@unisono.net.mx

La Calaca, folk art
Mesones #93, Col. Centro
San Miguel de Allende, Guanajuato 37700
52+415-152-3954 T
lacalacasm@hotmail.com

Capelo, ceramics
Alfarería Mayólica de Guanajuato
Cerro de la Cruz s/n, Mineral de Valenciana
Guanajuato, Guanajuato 36240
52+473-732-8964 T
ceramicapelo@prodigy.net.mx

Cerámica La Cruz, ceramics
Cerro de la Cruz s/n, Mineral de Valenciana
Guanajuato, Guanajuato 36240
52+473-732-6010 T and F
cercruz@hotmail.com

Fábrica de Talavera La Corona, ceramics
Máximo Rojas #2, Barrio de Santiago
San Pablo del Monte, Tlaxcala 90940
52+222-282-0080 T and F
www.fabricalacorona.com
tacorona@prodigy.net.mx

Galería Indigo, folk and fine art
Calle Allende #107, Col. Centro
Oaxaca, Oaxaca 68000
52+951-514-3889 T, 951-514-8338 F
galeriaindigosma@hotmail.com

Gorky Gonzáles, ceramics
Alfarería Tradicional
Ex-Huerta de Montenegro, Col. Pastita
Guanajuato, Guanajuato 36090
52+473-731-0389 T, 52+473-731-0462 F
in U.S. 415-738-6140
gorkyglz@prodigy.net.mx
www.gorkypottery.com

Guajuye, handblown glassware
Lupita #2, Col. Estación del Ferrocarríl
San Miguel de Allende, Guanajuato 37759
52+415-152-7030 T, 52+415-153-5444 F
info@guajuye.com
www.guajuye.com

Holler and Saunders, Ltd., interior design
P. O. Box 2151
Nogales, AZ 85628-2151
520-287-5153 T, 520-287-7133 F
hsltd2000@theriver.com

La Mano Mágica, folk art
M. Alcalá #203, Col. Centro
Oaxaca, Oaxaca 68000
52+951-516-4275 T and F
in U.S. 310-455-6085
info@lamanomagica.com
www.lamanomagica.com

Materiales Traqui, cement tiles
Calle 21 #74, x14 y16
Ucu, Yucatán 97357
52+988-916-1500 T, 52+988-916-1501 F
traquin84@prodigy.net.mx

Mayólica Santa Rosa, ceramics
KM 13 Carretera GTO-DH
Santa Rosa de Lima, Guanajuato 36330
52+473-102-5017 T, 52+473-102-5018 F
mayolicasantarosa@yahoo.com.mx

Mobili Piave, wood and furniture
Curtidurias #313, Col. Jalatlaco
Oaxaca, Oaxaca 68080
52+951-501-6120 T, 951-515-4399 F
rrelizondo@terra.com.mx
www.mobilipiave.com

Ojo de Venado, folk art
Plaza Valenciana s/n, Mineral de Valenciana
Guanajuato, Guanajuato 36240
52+473-734-1435 T
ojodevenado2001@yahoo.com

La Quinta de San Antonio, antiques
7 Oriente #215-5, Barrio de los Sapos
Puebla, Puebla 72000
52+222-232-1189 T
laquintadesanantonio@hotmail.com

Talavera Amora, ceramics
Av. del Salvador #5, Rancho Santa Teresa
Dolores Hidalgo, Guanajuato 37800
52+418-185-9002 T and F
amoradisyests@prodigy.net.mx

Talavera Casa Celia, ceramics
5 Oriente #608, Barrio de los Sapos
Puebla, Puebla 72000
52+222-242-3663 T, 52+222-235-1891 F
casacelia@puebla.megared.net.mx

Talavera de la Reyna, ceramics
Camino a la Carcaña #2413, Recta a Cholula
Cholula, Puebla 72760
52+222-225-4182 T, 222-225-4058 F
talaveradelareyna@prodigy.net.mx
www.talaveradelareyna.com.mx

Taller el Portón, copper
Pino Suarez #69
Santa Clara del Cobre, Michoacán
52+434-343-0305 T, 52+434-343-0305 F
portonartesan@hotmail.com

Toh Boutique, ceramics
Hacienda Chichén Resort
Chichén Itzá, Yucatán 97751
52+999-924-4222 T, 52+999-924-5011 F
in U.S. 877-631-4005
info@haciendachichen.com
www.haciendachichen.com

Mario López Torres, reed sculpture
Tzumindi, Independencia #88
Ihuatzio, Michoacán 58442
52+434-344-0779 T, 52+434-344-0780 F
tzumindi@hotmail.com
www.patzcuarolake.com/tzumindi

Uriarte Talavera, ceramics
4 Poniente #911, Col. Centro
Puebla, Puebla 72000
52+222-232-1598 T, 52+222-232-2433
puebla@uriartetalavera.com.mx
www.uriartetalavera.com.mx

Zócalo, folk art
Hernández Macías #110, Col. Centro
San Miguel de Allende, Guanajuato 37700
52+415-152-0663 T and F
info@zocalotx.com
www.zocalotx.com

First and foremost, we wish to thank the owners, managers, and directors of the homes, inns, and museums whose kitchens are seen in these pages. Your house was our house for a time, and we thank you profoundly for your generosity, flexibility, patience, and fabulously good taste. Also, our sincere thanks to the owners and staff of the many hotels and homes where we were provided bed, breakfast, and so very much more during our many sojourns though Mexico while preparing this book. Your generosity made this project possible.

In San Cristóbal de las Casas: David and Nancy Orr of Casa Felipe Flores and Javiér Espinosa of Hotel Casavieja. In Cuernavaca: Patricia Edelen Garita of Casa Ahuilayan, Sally Sloan of the Robert Brady Museum, Juan Fenton and Ana Suarez of Hacienda San Gabriel de las Palmas, Juan Coral of Las Mañanitas. In Guanajuato: Jaye Johnson and Sharon Mendez of Casa Estrella and Hugo and Angélica Anaya of La Casa de Espíritus Alegres. In Mérida: David Sterling and Keith Heitke of Los Dos Cooking School and Guest House, Fritz Menzel and Werner Gross of Casa del Pocito, Salvador Reyes Ríos and Josefina Larraín of Casa Reyes-Larraín, Deborah LaChapelle of Casa Santana, Dev and Chuck Stern of Hacienda Petac, Pedro and Soledad Hernández of Hacienda Itzincab, and Belisa Barbachano-Gordon of Hotel Casa del Balam. In Mexico City: Ignacio Custodio, Hilda Trujillo, Ma. Eugenia de Lara, and Carlos Phillips Olmedo of the Museo de Frida Kahlo, Casa Azul, and Museo Dolores Olmedo Patiño and Martín Morales of Hotel Boutique Casa Vieja. In Oaxaca: Susana Trilling of Rancho Aurora, Rosa Blum and Henry Wangeman of Casa Jalatlaco, Cathy Lopez and David Sandler of Casa de Vino Tinto, Alejandro Ruiz of Casa Oaxaca, Fundación Cultural Rodolfo Morales. In Pátzcuaro and Morelia: Edward E. Holler III and Samuel L. Saunders of Casa Holler-Saunders, Victoria Ryan and Cynthia de la Rosa of Casa Encantada, Hector Bustamante of El Refugio en Pátzcuaro, and Nicolas de Ressiet of Villa Montaña Hotel and Spa. In Puebla: Antonio Ramirez and Alfonso Bonilla of La Quinta de San Antonio; Yolanda Ramos of Casa Ramos; Petronio Escamilla and the Ex-Convent of Santa Rosa; Museo de la Revolución Mexicana; Edith Palacios and the Casa de Alfeñique; Museo Amparo; and Leobardo Espinosa, Mariana Alonzo, and the entire wonderful staff of Mesones Sacristía de la Compañía and Sacristía Capuchinas. In San Miguel de Allende: Deborah Turbeville, Jack and Terry Reinhardt of Casa de Cinco Perros, Timoteo Wachter, Melena Skåtun, and Iza of Casa Areca, Butch and Ann Futch of Casa Chuparosa, Patia and Buddy Finkbeiner of Casa Hypatia, Bobby and Yolanda Walsh of Casa Gaudí, Joyce Aaron of Villa el Cerrito, Kelli Brown and Marcia Brown Bland of Hacienda Calderón, Patsy Dubois of Patsy's Place, Robert Waters of Susurro, Dianne Kushner and Susana Zermeño of Casa Luna Pila Seca and Casa Luna Quebrada, Martha Hyder and the superb staff of Quinta Quebrada. In Tlaquepaque: Vicente García and Felix Vidales and Villa del Ensueño.

We are grateful for the generous support of Aeromexico and Mexicana Airlines, who made our travels possible; special thanks to Fatima Alas and Margie Gostlya for all their assistance. Alejandro Cruz-Serrano, director of Sectur, the Mexican Tourist Board in Los Angeles, we thank you.

Kudos and thanks to A&I Color Lab in Santa Monica, California, for another job well done.

For favors large and small, support, brilliant ideas, great recipes, inspiration, and help when we needed it, muchas gracias to: Ana Argáez of Sectur Yucatán, Evita Avery of La Calaca, Sarah Balla, Faye Cupp, Sra. Ma. Auxilio Diaz Barriga de Guizar, Tom Ellison, Larry Friedman, Mary Jane Gagnier, Lisa Gahafer, Yolanda Garcia Caballero of the Instituto de Comunicación y Cultura in Oaxaca, Raul Gíl, Gerry Gill, Bruce Gordon, Sue Graziano, Jane Gregorius, Gabriela Gudiño, Deb and Rick Hall of Zócalo, Jennifer Hamilton, John Hill and Tim Young, Carol Hopkins, Gina Hyams, Diana Kennedy, Rachael Laudan, Robin and Michael Lynch of Salt of the Earth, Gemma Macouzet, Ana Elena Martínez, Monica Mastetta, la familia McNair, the Mendoza sisters of Restaurant Tlamanali, Liz and David Merrill, Ana Miya, Nancy Najera, Deborah Peacock, Elvira Pruneda, Carlos Riveros (our key to the city of Puebla), Marilyn Tausend, Dena Taylor, Carmen Titita Ramírez Degollado of El Bajío, Lisa Vickers of the U.S. Consulate in Mérida, Maestro Randy Walz of Ojo de Venado, Lynda Watson, Gerd Werner, and Roy Zuloaga.

With special thanks to Judith Bettelheim for the walk on the beach that inspired this book.

And to the wonderful team at Chronicle Books: art director Aya Akazawa, production coordinator Alan Watt, managing editor Doug Ogan, copy editor Mimi Kusch, and editor-extraordinario Lisa Campbell, we thank you all for your brilliant work.

M.L. AND E.E.M.